Praise for *The Serving Leader*

"Most leadership books speak to your mind.
but if you'll let it . . . it will also speak to your s
your leadership."
—Jim Mellado, President, Willow

The Serving Leader is a must-read for all who lead a. ... ... read. Jennings
Stahl-Wert have presented models of leadership that are both inspirational and
compelling. In a period when so many leaders fall short, *The Serving Leader* tells us
that this need not be. This book should be in the hands of all who lead others."
—**Rev. Dr. W. Wilson Goode, Sr.,** former Mayor, City of Philadelphia

"Your principles are right on and mirror what I have come to learn from years
of leadership in the university, in business, and in the military. I think you've
struck the right balance between providing leadership principles that can be
applied in many settings and pointing to deeper issues of the meaning of work
and of life. Well done!"
—**John B. Hirt, PhD,** Major General, United States Marine Corps

"We all think a lot about the higher purpose we have, but I, for one, have
struggled with articulating its application in a broader sense of my community
and business life. Thank you for so clearly laying out the relevance and
dimensions of servant leadership."
—**Deb Magness,** Executive Director, Marketing & Communications, David A.
Tepper School of Business, Carnegie Mellon University

"Jennings and Stahl-Wert have managed to capture the essence of Servant
Leadership and have packaged it into a delightful and entertaining book. This
book will be the standard in the leadership field for quite a while!"
—**Dr. Alistair M. Hanna,** Chairman, ALPHA USA, Former McKinsey and
Company Director

"The Serving Leader gets to the heart of the struggle so many leaders are facing—
how to live a life of true significance. I recommend this book to anyone who is facing Halftime and exploring the possibility of moving from success to significance."
—**Bob Buford,** Founder and Chairman, Leadership Network, author of *Halftime:
Changing Your Game Plan from Success to Significance*

"I see *The Serving Leader* as a book with very broad appeal—something for more than
the management bookshelves. This is not a quick how-to business book. It could be
a *Prayer of Jabez* class book."
—**Perry Pascarella,** author of *Purpose Driven Organization*

"*The Serving Leader* is a must-read for any leader who wants to build a
great organization."
—**Jim Dauwalter,** President and CEO; Stan Geyer, Chairman, Entegris, Inc.

THE KEN BLANCHARD SERIES

SIMPLE TRUTHS UPLIFTING THE VALUE OF PEOPLE IN ORGANIZATIONS

∎

The Referral of a Lifetime

The Networking System That Produces
Bottom-Line Results . . . Every Day!
Tim Templeton

The Serving Leader

5 Powerful Actions That Will Transform Your Team,
Your Business, and Your Community
Ken Jennings and John Stahl-Wert

Your Leadership Legacy

The Difference You Make in People's Lives
Marta Brooks, Julie Stark,
and Sarah Caverhill

Formula 2 + 2

The Simple Solution for Successful Coaching
Douglas B. Allen and Dwight W. Allen

The Serving Leader

5 Powerful Actions That Will Transform Your Team, Your Business, and Your Community

Ken Jennings
John Stahl-Wert

BERRETT-KOEHLER PUBLISHERS, INC.
San Francisco

Berrett-Koehler Publishers, Inc.
235 Montgomery Street, Suite 650
San Francisco, CA 94104-2916
Tel: (415) 288-0260   Fax: (415) 362-2512   www.bkconnection.com

Ordering Information
Quantity sales. Special discounts are available on quantity purchases by corporations, associations, and others. For details, contact the "Special Sales Department" at the Berrett-Koehler address above.
Individual sales. Berrett-Koehler publications are available through most bookstores. They can also be ordered direct from Berrett-Koehler: Tel: (800) 929-2929; Fax: (802) 864-7626; www.bkconnection.com.
Orders for college textbook/course adoption use. Please contact Berrett-Koehler: Tel: (800) 929-2929; Fax: (802) 864-7626.
Orders by U.S. trade bookstores and wholesalers. Please contact Publishers Group West, 1700 Fourth Street, Berkeley, CA 94710. Tel: (510) 528-1444; Fax: (510) 528-3444.

Berrett-Koehler and the BK logo are registered trademarks of Berrett-Koehler Publishers, Inc.

Printed in the United States of America

Berrett-Koehler books are printed on long-lasting acid-free paper. When it is available, we choose paper that has been manufactured by environmentally responsible processes. These may include using trees grown in sustainable forests, incorporating recycled paper, minimizing chlorine in bleaching, or recycling the energy produced at the paper mill.

Library of Congress Cataloging-in-Publication Data
Jennings, Ken (Kenneth R.)
  The serving leader : 5 powerful actions that will transform your
team, your business, and your community / Ken Jennings and John
Stahl-Wert; foreword by Ken Blanchard.
    p. cm. — (The Ken Blanchard series)
  Includes bibliographical references.
  ISBN 1-57675-265-8 (hardcover)
  ISBN 1-57675-308-5 (paperback)
    1. Leadership. 2. Management. 3. Teams in the workplace
I. Stahl-Wert, John. II. Title. III. Series.
HF57.7.J46 2003
658.4'092—dc21   2003045388

FIRST EDITION
08 07 06 05 04   10 9 8 7 6 5 4 3 2 1

Copyediting and proofreading by PeopleSpeak.
Book design and composition by Beverly Butterfield, Girl of the West Productions.

CONTENTS

This book is dedicated to the colleagues and clients who
have taught us and to "the armies of compassion" mustering
in every neighborhood for the restoration of our nation's soul.

Special dedication to Philadelphia's Amachi Initiative,
one magnificent demonstration among countless others of
how leaders behave when they choose to serve.

FOREWORD

Coauthor of *The One Minute Manager®, Empowerment Takes More
Than a Minute, Raving Fans®, Gung Ho!®, Whale Done!*
and *Full Steam Ahead!*

I am thrilled to have Ken Jennings and John Stahl-Wert's excellent book, *The Serving Leader,* as a part of the Ken Blanchard
Series. This book will challenge you to lead differently. I believe it will also cause you to want to live your life differently. It presents so beautifully the simple truths that uplift
the value of people.

That Ken Jennings and John Stahl-Wert would write
this book together is a testament to the surprising nature of
the book. On the surface, Ken and John could hardly be
more different. Ken is a hypervelocity management consultant in constant motion between multiple corporations.
John is an inner-city leader who generally stays put to work
with his diverse partners creating extraordinary results for
the people of one city.

But together they have crafted a singular message for
leaders in businesses, communities, churches, and nonprofit
organizations. From two very different life paths has come
a unified vision of leadership and an understanding of

human change that will make a lifelong difference for you and the people you lead and serve.

What sets this book apart most of all is the beauty and quality of the storytelling. Ken and John have brought us a moving story that you will not want to put down. An estranged son, his dying father, and a wonderfully diverse group of innovative leaders in business, volunteer organizations, and civic groups work together to grasp and illustrate the basic daily actions that make a Serving Leader.

While *The Serving Leader* is presented as a work of fiction, the leaders and organizations Ken and John depict are based on real situations, and the results that are described match the incredible results being achieved in real businesses and communities. At the end of the book, the authors introduce us to some of these real-life leadership miracle stories.

On one level, *The Serving Leader* is the most practical guide available to implementing servant leadership in your life and work. On a deeper level, it is a book about the journey of growth that every great leader must be willing to take.

It gives me a special satisfaction to introduce you to the beautiful and life-challenging work of two of my good friends. Enjoy this book and be encouraged. You were born to make a difference!

INTRODUCTION

This is a story about leadership: leadership in teams, businesses, and communities. It is also a story about personal growth and how good leaders become great leaders through their willingness to face and be changed by the greatest challenges of their lives.

The story comes out of our friendship with Mike Wilson. Mike is a man we both know well. He shows up everywhere in the businesses and neighborhoods we serve. The circumstances of place and vocation vary, but Mike is always there. As a leader, he's professionally talented and highly motivated to successfully reach his business and financial goals.

But Mike wants his life to be about more than success. He's searching for the deeper significance of his leadership and for the satisfaction of living a life of real purpose. In this deeper search, however, Mike often feels very unsuccessful; sometimes, he feels completely lost.

As we've shared this story with our friends, these questions usually arise: "Is Mike's story real? And if it is, where can I find him?" Here's the best answer we have: Mike's story is real. And the chances are reasonable that you'll find someone like him occupying the office next to yours. She rides on the train with you each morning. You pass him in the hallway every day. Glance up from your reading and look around; she might be sitting right there in the room with you now.

Perhaps it would be helpful to say a brief word here about the friendship out of which this story was born. We two at first glance appear to have little in common. Ken is a business consultant who resides in the flight matrix that connects the great urban centers of America, Europe, and Asia. John is a community leader who resides and works in one great city. By strategic design, he leaves that city and his citywide colleagues as infrequently as possible. Ken works with bottom-line business leaders, John with frontline community leaders. Ken's work focuses on the corporate sector, John's on the faith-based sector. In terms of space and time, Ken's work is space expansive and more time limited; John's is the other way around.

These differences aside, our lives are much the same. We both work with men and women like Mike Wilson every day. In whatever airport Ken lands and on whatever street John walks, Mike is there, trying to close the painful gap between his hard-working day and his persistent sense of unfulfilled purpose.

Since we're making introductions here, we may as well go one step further. We, too, are Mike Wilson. While the details may be fictional, at its deepest level Mike's story is real—and very true.

Perhaps you will recognize yourself in parts of this story, too. If so, then you are already on your way. We hope these pages will offer you some guidance as well as encouragement as you continue on the journey of both professional and personal growth that great leadership requires.

Mike Wilson's
Journal

THE FAST TRACK DIVERTED

Why am I sitting on this train? If I had taken a flight, I'd already be there. Instead, I've got four more hours to sit here and fume about what I've gotten myself into.

I feel like I'm eight years old again. Dad says, "Why don't you ride down on the train, Son! It'll give you a chance to think." And so I just *do* it. Like I've got time to sit for hours, thinking. Like I actually enjoy trains.

The thing about trains is this: trains only show you what you're passing, not where you're headed. Whatever you can see out the window is already old news. Been there. Regularly, the track bends enough that you can catch a glimpse of the journey ahead, but as soon as the train straightens its aim for the goal, you're left sitting in the back just watching stuff go past. An hour into this trip, I'm way past bored.

Scratch that last sentence. I'm not bored. And, truthfully, being stuck on this train is not what I'm really troubled about. What upsets me is the fact that I don't know what's waiting for me at the end of this track. And I'm afraid to find out. I'm deeply worried about Dad. I don't know how I'm going to pass so much time sitting here just with myself.

And more truth: I used to *like* trains. A lot. It's one of the memories I *do* have with Dad. One of the too-few memories. And that's what this is *really* about. Sitting here reminds me of so much that I've lost. So much!

There you have it, boss: a journal entry. I'd say I'm well on my way!

All right, Mike, enough time on the therapist's couch. Here's a thought: scratch it all out. I doubt Charlie wants to read the sorry ramblings of a lost son.

Please let my dad be okay!

Okay, new start. Official sounding.

Journal entry: "Background and Orientation."

Two months ago, Charlie gave me the assignment of building a new leadership development practice for our firm, working from our Boston headquarters. An MBA, ten years of management consulting assignments, experience with nearly fifty clients around the world—I had done it all with this in mind, the chance to take the lead. Thirty-eight years old. Heading the development of our firm's newest and most promising practice area. My life was right on track!

Our firm routinely gets involved with helping clients attack tough strategic problems, strengthen their operations, and improve profitability. Up until now, however, we have never directly focused our client services on building critical leadership capacity in organizations. As a firm, we have the access and reputation required to build a practice in the area, but I knew we did not have a good handle on the current best practices in leadership effectiveness. It became my mission to pull together a point of view on "leadership that really works," as Charlie put the challenge to us.

So I buried myself and my crew—the colleagues who joined me—in the research available about leadership, including traits, models, value propositions. PowerPoint presentations were zigzagging back and forth between our offices like crazed bats. We interviewed some of the best CEOs in the country, scanned mountains of journal articles, met with professors and writers who studied leadership, and amassed our data. We felt like we were launching a major Himalayan expedition. It felt good!

In all our research, some threads emerged. And a few especially puzzling findings spurred us to go deeper.

A Boulder, Colorado–based "freelance professor" and rock climber, Jim Collins, along with his team, had found some unusually curious data. He observed that dramatic improvements in company performance were coming from leaders whose traits and practices broke the traditional leadership mold. This research described leaders who were personally humble (in some cases, almost shy) and totally devoted to the service of others but who were also fiercely and unwaveringly resolved to do whatever it took to improve organizational performance. Something was jarring about great results coming from a self-effacing style, but the data was compelling.

It occurs to me just now that it was this Collins research that got me thinking again about my own dad as a leader. All right, score a point for this long train trip. Back in business school, I took a fair measure of ribbing about my famous father. He was featured in one of the school's management case studies about leadership, ethics, and decision making in business. Honestly, I didn't put much effort into that assignment. Dad was well known, admired by many, so loved. And he gave me, his son, so little of himself. It was a sore point. Still is.

I didn't fare very well on that particular assignment, and my classmates rode me big time. Not that I really cared; I figured back then that some of them were better suited to social work than business, anyway.

But reading Collins had caused me to reconsider all of this. What I've always heard about my dad's way of working sounds suspiciously like the profile of the effective leader Collins described. The thought had even crossed my mind that if I was going to launch a new leadership practice, then my old man might be helpful. Just a week ago I was thinking about Dad and wishing I could get past my hurt enough to reach out to him and run some of these ideas past him.

I should be more careful what I wish for. Mom called me on the same day I was having those thoughts.

"Hi, Son," Mom said. "I'm glad I caught you. Do you have a minute to talk?"

Her words were casual, but her voice had none of its normal breezy character. A feeling of alarm began to creep up the back of my neck. Of course I had a minute to talk!

"It's about your father," she continued more slowly. She cleared her throat. "I've been putting this conversation off for a while, Mike. He's not been feeling that great lately." Mom's voice cracked, and silence filled the line.

"Oh, just hand me the phone, Margaret!" My father's voice broke the silence with that tone of impatience I knew so well. He sounded all right to me.

"Look, Mike, things aren't too good right now. I met with my doctor this morning and there's a problem. The bottom line is that I'm going to have to cut back on some things. He wants me to get a little treatment. Rest up."

I was stunned. My mouth opened, but nothing came out. I had no words.

"I need your help, Mike," he continued, his voice suddenly sounding like a badly scratched record. "I'm involved in some leadership projects here, and they're all at critical points." Now it was Dad's turn to clear his throat. "I thought you could step in for me for a while, maybe a couple weeks," he finished weakly.

I wasn't processing any of this. My father, the master of understatement where his own personal issues are concerned, was saying that he had a problem! He needed a little treatment!

"I've talked about this with your boss. He told me you're launching the firm's leadership practice, so this should benefit both of us." Dad plowed on with his pitch like a runner determined to hit the finish line. "While you're helping us out, the team here will teach you what we've learned about a unique approach to leadership. Charlie suggested you keep a journal on your investigations while you're here, and I've got some friends who can help you develop it into something useful later." I heard my father take a quick breath.

"Would you come and help me, Son? Please?"

And just like that, my leadership sabbatical began. I can't adequately express how strange it is that I made such an abrupt move. I was in the middle of everything I had always wanted, on the threshold of a future I had always dreamed of. And I didn't like my father's unsolicited intervention with my boss in the least. Back to my earlier comment about feeling eight years old.

And yet I didn't hesitate. The sound of Mom's voice. What my dad said. What I felt in my heart. It all just went "click."

The next day, I handed off assignments to my crew. I decided to leave my techno-gadgets at home, packing three blank notebooks and an anxious mind. At the last minute, on an impulse, I dug back through my graduate school files and grabbed the case study on my pop. I was going to see him, yet I still didn't really know who he was.

My executive assistant booked me a seat on Amtrak to Philly for the very next day. She looked at me suspiciously, like I'd lost my mind. Amtrak! I explained myself by repeating my dad's explanation: "It'll give me time to think." Her frown worsened—it was alien possession, not mere mental distress.

And here I am. I spent the first forty-five minutes of my trip reviewing Dad's case study and have been writing ever since. I'm beginning to suspect that this investigation may well be as much about him as his projects. I'm actually glad. It's time.

Some notes from my reading:

The son of a coal miner, my dad grew up in tough circumstances. Like many of his generation, he went to war when called. On Robert Wilson's twentieth birthday, a cease-fire was signed in Korea's Panmunjom, and he was shipped home. The GI Bill took him to Princeton where, according to the case study, he ran track. That reminded me of my favorite photo of him. A boyish Robert Wilson is straining forward, chest first, breaking the tape 100 yards ahead of the field in a 100-yard race! So fiercely determined was he to win that he false-started, failed to hear the recall gun, and ran the entire race alone. He explained to me, "I always expect to win and never look back to see the other guys."

That's the dad I know.

But the case study drew another picture that didn't fit this first-at-all-costs photo. Starting his career as a pharmaceutical salesman and rising quickly to management, he distinguished himself as a team builder. He always credited the team with his success, the file declared, and appeared to be genuinely surprised whenever he received recognition or promotions.

This just doesn't square with what I thought I knew about him. Honestly, I never felt that he gave me credit for much of anything.

Robert Taylor Wilson was described in the article as unique. When he became CEO of the company twenty-two years later, he hardly ever stayed in his office (or at home, I might just add). He spent a lot of time in activity that looked more like teaching than managing. He practically turned his company's entire senior team into teachers.

As a leader, he was known for setting high goals and standards. He was death on what the article called "mistakes of the heart," poor ethical decisions like when managers shaded the truth, took credit when it belonged to others, or passed on unflattering remarks about their colleagues. Conversely, he was softer on other kinds of mistakes. He used honest missteps as teaching occasions. He encouraged risk taking, though he wasn't afraid to remove people for persistent underperformance. His top leadership team actually got smaller in his first few years, even as the company doubled in size and profitability.

He avoided taking credit when things were going well; indeed, he went to great pain to attribute success to others. At the corporate annual meeting, he always showcased others' accomplishments, not his own.

He called himself a "truth teller." He was famous for plain talk, for going to great lengths to describe company performance accurately. This part, at least, I recognize. He also encouraged managers to honestly describe the reality of their unit's performance.

Reviewing all of this from my dad's corporate past, I am becoming very curious to see the leadership system he has helped build in Philly. Maybe more to the point, I think I'm ready to take a fresh look at my father, give us both another chance.

Robert Taylor Wilson. I know that he looks great on paper. I know he has hundreds of loyal friends. I know that people love working for him. I also know there are dimensions of this man that I've never encountered. And I think I'd like to.

While I'm chronicling things I know, here's one more. I know why I'm sitting on this train. My father said "please." It wasn't "Get down here, Son!" Just "please." I don't remember ever hearing that before.

Okay, time to put the pen down and watch America go past my window. The ride might not be too bad, really. I'm noticing the track bending out ahead. I can see the engine now, but even so, I can't see where it's heading. I suppose that if I were seated with the conductor at the head of this train, I would still be unable to see what's around that bend.

I wonder where this journey will take me.

A NEW ASSIGNMENT

Day's end, and what a day it has been. Mom and Dad are in bed, and I'm back in my boyhood bedroom feeling time warped and badly torn between feelings of exhilaration and grief. I've got to somehow capture this incredible and tumultuous day.

Amtrak's *Acela Express* pulled into Philly's Thirtieth Street station at 12:05, five long hours after my Boston departure. Wanting to stretch my legs, I hiked the short thirteen blocks east along Market, crossing the majestic Schuylkill River—the Manayunk, as I insisted it be called in my boyhood Indian phase—to my first appointment of the day.

Dad had arranged for me to plunge right in with a lunch meeting at the famous Pyramid Club, high atop my hometown's new, art deco skyline. When I walked in, I was stunned by the gaunt and pale face that greeted me, my dad's wan smile masking nothing of the seriousness of his condition. He must have lost thirty pounds, and that from a frame that had been quite trim to begin with.

Dad saw that I noticed. Not giving me a chance to comment, he hooked my elbow and steered me to a circle of six men and women standing to the side. I saw the unspoken apologies on their faces—they already knew what Dad would put off telling me for another five hours.

Relocated to our table, my lunch mates introduced themselves. The first three were chief executive officers. One was the CEO of a premier biotech firm, the second had spent her career in financial services, and the third came out of the manufacturing industry. Next was the city's former mayor, Dr. Will Turner, now devoted to the work of his inner-city church. Will said a few words about his passion for the city and for serving the most vulnerable members of the community.

Another member was an academic, Martin Goldschmidt. Martin was a sociologist whose research was aimed at understanding why some social sector initiatives succeeded and why others failed so miserably.

The final member was a transplanted Irishman named Alistair Reynolds. "Ali" was known to me already, but by reputation only. He'd had a meteoric stint with my firm prior to my own tenure there. Ali described himself as a "social entrepreneur." I had heard the term before but never actually met one. Social entrepreneurs, by definition, approach social sector needs with entrepreneurial and capital-generating strategies. He could have used his talents to continue making many millions for the firm and plenty for himself, but he had set that goal aside. Strange.

Dad also indicated that there were other members of the team not at the lunch. I wondered how such an interesting and diverse group wound up working together.

After the introductions, Ali stood up. "Mike, we'd like to tell you why we are here. Actually, we chose this spot because we want to show you. Dr. Turner," he continued, "would you do the honors?"

So right there in the Pyramid Club, we all got up and followed Turner to the windows looking south over Philadelphia. He turned to me and said, "Up here, you can practically see the whole city. When our team first started to meet, we'd come here for lunch, look out at the city, and talk about its challenges. Looking here to the south," he continued, "you'll see growing businesses, the airport, the seaport, and a network of diverse neighborhoods." He went on to outline the team's projects on the south side of town. "Follow me," he said, speaking with a gracious authority. I followed.

As we walked, he expanded on his points. "As a team, we concluded that one of the most significant barriers to progress in all sectors of the city was the lack of effective leadership. We have been working for several years to accelerate the emergence of effective leaders around the city. We are now working in all sectors of the city: business, government, nonprofit, and community organizations.

"If you look out into the distance," Turner continued, "you can almost make out some of the homes, churches, and businesses in what we call the Main Line. There are exciting stories waiting there for you, Mike."

On around the building we continued, with everyone getting a chance to talk. We spent the better part of an hour walking around the club, eventually coming back to our table.

During lunch, Dad didn't eat. Frankly, I was torn between the exhilarating ideas I was hearing about and the grief that was welling up within me. There was nothing I could do about any of this. Ali had resumed the position of lead and just kept plowing forward with his narration.

"Let me shift focus from our projects to our team, Mike," Ali said. "So, who are we? We call ourselves the No-Name Team." Laughing at my puzzled expression, he continued. "It's a little contrived, but we're not the story, and we want to make that clear. The leaders who are out on the frontline are the story. They're the ones who make the difference, and we're here to support them.

"We really think we have something quite remarkable going on here. You'll see that there have been some amazing breakthroughs. Individuals, teams, and organizations have accomplished much more than any of us thought possible. We've seen for-profit companies accelerate past their peers, nonprofit organizations work much more effectively, and churches have gotten their members off the pews and into high-impact work in the community. Even our friends in the government are improving.

"A new kind of leader is getting this done. That's the bottom line."

I noticed that one of our waitresses was standing off to the side, her ear cocked to hear Ali's remarks, her head nodding in agreement. She'd been listening!

He continued. "We believe the key to success is what we call 'the Serving Leader.'"

"So you're basing your approach on the writings about servant leadership," I said. "On Robert Greenleaf and others." This growing body of work had been part of my team's research.

"Well, yes and no," Ali responded. "Yes, we've all read Greenleaf and with him Blanchard, Tichy, Collins, Block, Bennis, Gallup, Wheatley, Senge, Kotter, Drucker, and much of everything else that's been written in the field."

"I've read it all, too!" I interjected, wanting everyone to know I was pretty much up to speed. "Great stuff!"

"It's all great, Mike!" He sounded irritated. "Greenleaf and the great thought leaders who have followed him pioneered such important thinking about leadership. They have helped transform our basic assumptions about what makes great leadership great.

"But I also have to tell you, no! We're not basing our approach just on writings and books. Mike," he continued, his voice softer now and more imploring, "we've learned so much on the ground here, from Serving Leaders who are in the trenches with their teams, businesses, and neighborhoods *doing* what everyone's writing about. Our emphasis here is on what a leader actually does to support individuals, teams, and organizations. This is why we use the active word *serving*. The *theory* of servant leadership is vital, but it's the *active Serving Leader* who makes the critical difference."

I glanced over at my dad and saw the greatest look of satisfaction I think I've ever seen on his face. Dad was pleased with Ali—and with what Ali was saying—and his face left no room for doubt. I could sure stand to see that expression pointing in my direction sometime.

Dad caught me looking at him and nodded his head once. "Ali's gotten right to the point," he said. "And here's your first hint: the Serving Leader has a way of helping everyone else to succeed. Almost before we've spotted a Serving Leader, we notice this symptom—people all around are flourishing."

"So here's your task in a nutshell, Mike," Ali said. "Look at what we show you and then write the story. Put to work all that fine consulting expertise your dad is always bragging about."

I glanced over at Dad again. He was cleaning his glasses. He didn't glance back.

Ali was still talking. "We want you to make simple and practical sense of what the Serving Leader is doing that causes teams and companies and communities to flourish. Make it teachable, Mike. Make it learnable."

I just blinked. How was I going to do that?

Seeing my dubious expression, Ali laughed. "We're going to do this together," he said encouragingly. "Why don't we start by making a picture."

He took his napkin, placed it on the table between us, and drew a pyramid. Then he spun the napkin, flipping the pyramid upside down.

"I think you'll see that this Serving Leader approach takes almost all of our thinking on leadership and turns it right up on its head. At least since the pharaohs, we've thought of leadership as climbing to the top of the pyramid, right? I mean, here we sit at the top of the Pyramid Club, just like leaders are supposed to."

I nodded, though I can't say I was totally thrilled by what I was hearing. Being able to dine at the Pyramid Club is cool. Climbing is what my life's been largely about, truth be told.

The Serving Leader is down here unleashing the strengths, talents, and passions of those he or she serves. It works this way for a team of two, a business with a thousand employees, or a community of several million.

"Our findings point us in another direction," Ali continued. "The Serving Leader is down here at the bottom of the picture. The team, the business, and even the entire community are up above. The Serving Leader is down here unleashing the strengths, talents, and passions of those he or she serves. It works this way for a team of two, a business with a thousand employees, or a community of several million. Quite a switch, huh?"

Quite!

Ali shoved the napkin over to me, and I just stared at it. A plain, upside-down pyramid hand-drawn on a simple paper napkin. This was my starting point. Candidly, I was expecting more, but conscious of all the eyes upon me, I reached out and retrieved my gift. Okay. It was a starting point. I gave it a good look, folded it up, and tucked it into my coat pocket.

Glancing up again, I saw Ali nod his satisfaction to my father. What he was satisfied with, I don't know. That I had picked up his little picture and put it into my pocket? Very impressive!

I must confess that as I recount this day, I'm feeling overwhelmed. But I'm getting ahead of myself. Let me finish my first day's account.

The rest of the lunch went by quickly. Each team member agreed to a schedule of time with me. My time with each of them was to be spent focusing on their key projects. I was to learn both by observation and by rolling up my sleeves to work on some of the projects.

Clearly, they were excited about having me involved. I was more than a little nervous about all of this. I kept glancing over at my dad to see what was registering on his face. Ali had spoken of my father's pride in me. I wanted to see his pride firsthand. Dad didn't return my glances.

After lunch, Dad suggested I come with him. Much to my surprise, the elevator doors opened to the lobby and there stood my boss, Charlie, like he was expecting us! "Hey, Mike! How's it going?" Charlie said.

"Hey, Charlie," I answered. I glanced over at my dad. There was no surprise on his face. I shook my head. Dad was up to more than met the eye, and I wasn't enjoying it.

"I was in town and wanted to see how your old man is doing," Charlie explained.

Plausible, but not satisfactory. Dad was maneuvering me. He wasn't relating to me. He still hadn't told me *anything*.

They moved ahead of me and talked quietly. It was strange to see my boss supporting my dad with his arm as we walked to the street.

In the cab, I steered the conversation to my task. "This Serving Leader thing would seem to be a stretch for real business applications," I began. "It might work in social sector projects, but it's hard to imagine us selling something like this to our clients."

"Far from it, actually," my boss said. "I really think we need something fresh. More to the point, I think you're going to see approaches that deliver more than the old paradigms do. I want you to examine these Serving Leader approaches. Your father is quite excited about what's going on, and he's as tough a grader as there is."

No argument from me on this score.

"My instinct tells me this thing could indeed be commercial. That's one of the reasons you're here, Mike."

I was getting anxious. This was clearly not going to be the quick and simple proposition Charlie seemed to think. I was going to have to work my way through a jumbled smorgasbord of diverse projects—even diverse worlds. The worlds of the corporation, the nonprofit, the neighborhood, and the government.

And through it all, I was going to have to find simple, teachable principles that Charlie assumed would then sell new business like hotcakes. I wasn't sure which challenge was the more daunting, connecting all of the scattered dots I was shown at lunch or reconnecting with my father. This was not going to be a quick little detour from my nicely arranged life.

Dad directed the cab to deliver Charlie to the airport and then to take us home. After Charlie left us, I asked Dad to tell me how he was doing. "Later" was all he'd say.

What else should I write? Mom and Dad and I had dinner at home, an old boyhood favorite from my mother's Pennsylvania Dutch past—shepherd's pie. And, again, Dad barely nibbled at the edge of his serving.

I could weep, there's so much hitting me, so many things coming at me all at once. I've lost so much, left so many things behind. Too many things.

And now I know the very worst of it. I had just pushed back my plate when Dad said it. A few spare, chosen words, and my world will never be the same.

"It's pancreatic, Son," he said simply, evenly. "Too far gone to treat."

Just that. My dad will die this summer. I have to write it again, it's so hard to grasp. My dad will die this summer.

So here I am, back in my boyhood room, trying to capture my day on paper. A noisy owl calls out in the dusk. No other sounds. Okay, Mike, start with what you have—a napkin, a picture, some words, a very heavy heart.

Assignment notes:

- Learn what Serving Leaders do and how their approach works.
- Use the upside-down pyramid to structure what I learn.
- Be with my dad while he dies.

I don't know if I can do this!

ACTION: UPEND THE PYRAMID

"Look, Son," Dad said at breakfast this morning, "I know that you and I need to talk. I know it," he repeated, making sure that I heard him.

Dad really looked at me when he said this, his eyes revealing what they usually keep hidden, a depth of love for me and his understanding of my need. We'd talk. My dad and I would not miss our chance.

"But today, Mike," he continued, "I want you to go to work. Dive in, Son! Please!"

There it was again. "Please." I just looked at him for a moment, trying to get my bearings. Dad and I were going to make a connection—that's what he just promised. Underneath everything else, that's all I really wanted.

But right now seemed as good a time as any to start that talk. It's not like we have all the time in the world, right? And there have been other promises—ball games he wouldn't miss, the speech I was going to give at my high school graduation. He'd get there in time, he had promised.

"Okay, Dad," I said, nodding my head. It wasn't okay. But I wasn't ready, either, truth be told. I wasn't ready to go to that place I would need to go when we had our talk. Everything was too upside down. The news of last night was too fresh, my torn feelings of love and hurt too jumbled. So, I'd go to work today. I'd try to please, like he asked. It's familiar ground.

"Ali's got a big day for you," Dad then said, his face looking relieved. "He drew you an upside-down pyramid yesterday. Today you'll visit with some leaders who've up-ended the pyramid—and are making an incredible difference."

I pulled Ali's napkin out of the inside cover of my notebook, smoothed it out in front of me, and penned my father's words onto the picture.

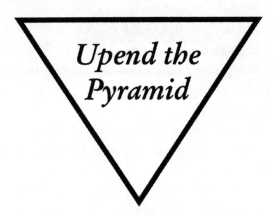

I clicked my pen closed and looked up from my note. I could focus on a task with the best of them. "Okay, Dad," I repeated, "but first a question. You've been at this for a while. Why don't you head me in the right direction this morning by giving me your definition of a Serving Leader?" I was ready to engage, now. And deep inside, I believed my dad. We *would* talk!

Dad smiled at me, his eyes again soft. I could really get used to my dad looking at me this way.

"I could answer your question," he began. "But I believe the best answers will come to you from your own observations of the leaders you're going to meet. Let their lives speak to you. I can always give you my view later."

I glanced over at my mom. My dad didn't have a lot of "later" to work with. She was looking at my dad with a little twist of a smile on her face and tears in her eyes.

"All right," I answered, returning my attention to him. "I'll head out with my eyes open. But, Dad," I continued, "I hope our talk is going to be sooner rather than later."

Another quick glance at Mom told me she had the same hope.

"Fair enough, Son," Dad replied. "We'll make it sooner. In fact, let's make a small start right now."

I clicked my pen right back open.

"Serving Leaders are living paradoxes. They create results by doing some rather counterintuitive things. I want you to look for the paradoxes. Find the paradoxes and you'll find the principles."

I paused a moment to absorb his comment.

"Can you give me one example? Point me in the right direction?"

"One example. Serving Leaders upend the pyramid. That's what you just wrote down. Now here's the paradox. You qualify to be first by putting other people first."

I just stared at him, waiting for his words to make sense.

"Write it down," he added, smiling and pointing to my notebook.

I wrote it down.

You qualify to be first by putting other people first.

"You're going to be seeing new things, Mike. Or seeing in a new way. To do that you're going to need new eyes."

Dad and I just looked at each other. This was *already* new—Dad and me looking at each other. I have no idea how to get new eyes, but my dad's looking at me gives me real hope.

"I have a date with your mom today!" he said. "You should probably get going yourself."

One more glance at Mom showed the clouds of worry that were in her eyes.

Outside it was one of those glorious, clear summer days. In the car with Ali, I pulled out my journal. "While you're driving, why don't you tell me the story of your life?"

"It's a long and sorry story," Ali began with a laugh. "Actually, from what I hear, it's not all that different from your own."

I got the joke and smiled back.

Ali started again. "I came to the States after an education in math and physics. I went to business school in Boston. After B-school, I joined the firm in the strategy practice. Those were the early days of the firm. Like you, I did a lot of studies and even wrote a few books. But at one point, I hit a defining moment. I led a firmwide review to find the best results achieved by clients through our consulting efforts."

"I read that report," I interrupted him. "All my crew working on our new leadership services offering read it. It was good!"

"Thanks," Ali said, "but at the time our findings were more than a little disturbing to the firm. As you now know, the best predictor of business results in studies of our clients was not *our* firm's brilliant strategies. It was the quality of *their* leadership. This made me very curious, and I took pains to learn all I could about leadership in our successful clients' companies. In my last years at the firm, I tried to weave more focus on leadership development into our engagements."

"Right. Your engagements are still being talked about in the firm. You had quite a string of successes."

"Thanks again," he said with a boyish smile that took years off his face. "As you know, the firm has a 'dog-eat-old-dog' culture. It eventually became time for me to step down. My regret was that I had not further developed the leadership initiative I had started at the firm. Maybe you will do that.

"Actually," Ali continued, his face suddenly very sober. "I have bigger regrets than what I didn't complete." He let the comment hang for a moment before continuing. "I almost lost my marriage over those years. All the work. All the stress. I'm thankful we were able to repair the damage, but I'll never get those years back. I'm sorry, Mike. I just remembered your own situation."

I shook my head. It's a subject I don't like to think about. Susan left me ten years ago. She's been married to her new husband longer now than she was to me. They have children. I don't really think about it much anymore. I make a point of trying not to think about it. And I can't say that I understand what happened. We loved each other. We got married. Then she left.

"I didn't mean to take you back there," Ali said, interrupting my private pang.

"It's okay," I answered. It wasn't.

"So after the firm, I moved here to live and to run my own consulting business. And then one day, your father called."

I returned my attention from my old pain to Ali's story.

"Your dad knew of my interest in leadership so he suggested I take a late-midlife leap and join him. He assigned me as a consultant to project leaders here in the city, and I've been at it now for several years. We'll visit two such projects this morning."

"It sounds like you haven't really changed jobs at all."

"Oh, but I have! I have definitely changed jobs. This is more significant than anything I've done before. You'll see. I genuinely love the people I'm serving. And I'm having a lot more fun in my second half of life."

"Tell me what we're going to see."

"Our first stop is at an amazing organization, run by an even more remarkable leader, Dorothy Hyde. From the outside, it looks like an ordinary factory. The organization is called Aslan Industries, and it's an outrageously successful enterprise right in the heart of the inner city. Wait until you see what's on the inside.

"Aslan started out as an after-school tutoring program. The leadership team there understood, though, that poor grades and delinquency were just symptoms of the problems in this part of the city. One of the root causes was a lack of career opportunities. Why prepare for a future if you aren't going to have one? So they concluded that Aslan had to do something about job readiness for promising jobs. They had to build a job-training organization.

"However, they knew nothing about job training. Since they didn't know enough to know what couldn't be done, they did the impossible. They built one of the most effective job-training programs for machinists in the region, and while they're doing this training, they're also running a very productive machine shop right here in the neighborhood.

Every year their excellent reputation in the shipyards wins them more business.

"I'd be willing to bet that you've rarely seen such an effective organization as Aslan," Ali added. "And I'll also bet that you're unlikely to have met a leader like Dorothy Hyde."

As we drove, I began to notice the neighborhoods change. At first boarded-up houses were rare. Then they became the norm. I even saw a few burned-out ones. How could a first-class training and manufacturing organization function here?

Suddenly, we drove into a block of beautifully refurbished industrial buildings. A sharply dressed and smiling guard waved us into a parking area right in front of a renovated factory building.

Dorothy Hyde met us at the door of her office. She stood about five feet nothing, a bundle of enthusiasm in a business suit. She greeted Ali with a grandmotherly embrace and then, to my great surprise, treated me to the same unpretentious ritual. Would milk and cookies follow? I wondered.

"Mike, it's good to meet you," Dorothy began. "Let's take a little walk around the office. You'll be seeing the manufacturing complex and classrooms later. Follow me!"

We fell in line behind Dorothy. As we walked, she introduced us to every person we met, each time relating a story about that person's recent contributions to the training and job creation mission of Aslan. They all beamed as Dorothy spoke of them and would then add a word or two of information. Every encounter included an introduction, a story, some praise, and even some planning, all of it right before our eyes! By the time we reached her office, she had worked meaningfully with nearly a dozen people. I was in total awe! How many times have I followed an executive into a factory and watched as the workers glanced away or pretended to be too busy to notice? The difference here was stunning.

In the conference room, Dorothy told me the story of Aslan. "I guess you're wondering how a housewife and grandmother like me winds up here."

I nodded. I *was* wondering this.

"It goes back to some of this city's darkest days," Dorothy explained. "In our frustration and anger over our poverty and lack of opportunity, we were literally destroying our neighborhoods and ourselves. I couldn't stand it any longer. I didn't feel suited to the task, but I was convinced that we had to turn our situation around. So I got to work, and others joined me."

Dorothy went on to describe an amazing story of birth, growth, significance, and success. Her own training in book-keeping years earlier at Howard University had been buried under the press of life—children, struggles with the local schools, her husband's cyclical unemployment, and the daily chores of stretching resources as far as possible to make ends meet.

She had grown through it all, winning the trust of her neighbors through diligent concern for all the children on her street. She had gained the respect of the high school principal by bringing parents together to assist with much-needed hall monitoring. She had become an asset to her local councilman by consistently addressing the most urgent neighborhood topics with a positive focus. When Dorothy pointed out a problem, she also offered several solutions, and she always showed up when it was time to do the hard work of implementation.

Hers was a natural progression into leadership. Better to say she had been growing into a leader long before anyone thought to call her one. Hall monitoring became after-school tutoring. When the school tutoring center needed computers, Dorothy dusted off her old training and wrote the budget for a grant request. Seeing her thoroughness, the principal asked her to write the whole proposal, which she promptly did, with success. Gaining this success through her volunteer work at the high school led her naturally to look at issues of job readiness after graduation. She had already gotten to know some local funders and returned to them to pitch a job-training pilot program. Feasibility money made it possible to do a broad market-and-needs analysis. Opportunities were identified, and both the foundation community and the private sector figured out that they could advance their own interests by partnering with Dorothy. She helped them figure this out.

"What we have here," Dorothy was explaining, "is a people development engine. On the demand side, we did our homework with the businesses in this area. We discovered that Philadelphia was facing a critical shortage of skilled machinists. We went to shops all over the city and throughout the shipyards, hundreds of them, and asked them if they would be willing to take machinists of color if we trained them. A deal shaped up. If we could produce great machinists, both in terms of skill and reliability, these shops would have plenty of jobs available.

"I just knew," Dorothy continued, her voice as full and emphatic as a preacher at full thunder, "that we could do it! No one could tell me that our trainees could not become the very best of the best. So I focused all my energy on our students' success. Their success was my success!

"From a leadership standpoint. I had to redefine the concept of 'being in charge.' I'm not in charge so much as I'm committed to whatever causes my followers to *get* charged. *Charged up,* that is."

I wrote it down.

You're in charge principally to charge up others.

In fact, I wrote down as much as I possibly could. Two hours later, I had filled many pages with stories of success and of changed lives. Aslan lives out Dorothy's commitment to charge up people. What makes the team at Aslan great is the greatness its students achieve.

Dorothy finally took a break. "I want you to talk with my chief operating officer, Harry Donohue," she said. "He's a retired chief master sergeant who is now deep into what we call his 'second-half' career." With that, she left us to find her COO.

"What a remarkable woman!" I said to Ali.

"No argument. Tell me what you learned this morning."

"Dorothy is fantastically focused on business results, but at the same time, she was persistent in pointing out the individual contributions of each person. Except in the case of herself."

"Right," said Ali. "I really wanted you to notice that. A defining characteristic of a Serving Leader that you will see again and again around here involves the issue of *ego*. You saw it with Dorothy, and I think you'll see it in every one of our leaders. They direct the credit to others. Dorothy is constantly getting her ego out of the way and building up others."

"So people end up feeling good about themselves."

"Well, that's true. But it's not the most important point. Self-esteem is very important because it sets up a powerful cycle of personal growth, willingness to take risks, persistence, and results. But getting your ego out of the way has an even deeper organizational impact."

I wasn't sure what Ali was getting at, but I was definitely listening.

"The Serving Leader handles his or her own ego," Ali continued, "because the best results come from genuine teamwork. The leader turns the pyramid onto its head in order to serve others. When a leader keeps personal ego in check—and builds the confidence and self-esteem of others—it is then possible for the team to work together."

> When a leader keeps personal ego in check—and builds the confidence and self-esteem of others—it is then possible for the team to work together.

"You're saying that if a leader models the importance of building up others and doesn't care about getting the credit for the achievement, other members of the team will do the same thing."

"Exactly," Ali said. "By putting others first in this way, the Serving Leader is able to catalyze the creation of high-performance teams."

As we finished, former Chief Master Sergeant Donohue strode in, his spit-polished black shoes snappily striking the hardwood floor with rhythmic precision. I felt my spine straightening involuntarily.

"Harry Donohue," he said briskly. "I'm your tour guide. So fall in."

"Yes, sir," I nearly barked, rising to do as instructed.

"Not 'sir.' Harry," Donohue corrected gruffly. "I work for a living!"

Startled, I glanced quickly over at Ali, who was trying to suppress a very happy expression.

Our first visit was to a classroom where basic skills in math and English were being taught. Harry introduced us to students as we went along, acting exactly as Dorothy had. He gave us remarkable statistics on graduation rates, as well as illustrations of student confidence being built and skills being acquired. The whole place was as neat as a pin, every wall covered with motivational quotations and symbols of achievement. No military barracks awaiting inspection had ever looked neater.

"Would you tell me what the secrets of success are here, Harry?" I began.

"I don't know about secrets," he replied. "I put the students first. I still get up at 4:30 every morning to be here before the students arrive. I enforce the rules. If you miss class twice, you're out. If you sleep in class, you're out. Drugs or other substances, you're out. If you don't get the grades, we offer you as much assistance as you can stand. But if you can't or won't make the grade, sadly, you're out.

"Life is a high-wire act," he continued. "We do not coddle the students. That simply doesn't serve them well. We believe in their capacity for strength and determination, and they tend to rise to those expectations. They have to stay on the wire to succeed."

I said, "The thing I started to see here was the way your leaders put the students above themselves. I'm calling this 'Upend the Pyramid.' You and Dorothy and the other leaders move to the bottom of the pyramid and work to charge up the students."

Harry nodded once.

"But now I'm realizing that something else is going on that's very different, something that almost seems contradictory. On the one hand, you're serving people, but on the other hand, you've got really tough standards! How does that fit together?"

Harry opened his mouth to answer, but Ali cut him off. "Sorry to disappoint you, Mike, but your question will get an answer at our next stop. And we're already late."

I was disappointed. I felt I was only getting started with Harry. I thanked him for his time and promised a prompt return visit. He said he would welcome that, and I felt that he really meant it.

"Harry," I thought to ask, just as we were about to leave the room, "how did you meet Dorothy?"

Harry's war-tempered, ramrod, tough-guy persona transformed right in front of my eyes. I might have been watching a cop newly home from his punishing beat as he slumps, gratefully, into his favorite chair. Every guard was lowered.

"She saved my kid," Harry answered simply, his eyes level with mine. In this moment, I wasn't looking at former Chief Master Sergeant and Taskmaster Extraordinaire Harry Donohue. I was looking at somebody's dad.

I nodded my head in acknowledgment. I want to spend more time with this man.

"I can see why you love this place," I said to Ali as we walked back to the parking lot. "Their accomplishments are remarkable. How do they pull it off?"

"Hold the analysis for just a second," Ali interrupted. "What did you *feel* here?"

I stopped in my tracks and raised my hands, palms facing forward toward the factory building. I closed my eyes. "I feel the power," I said, poking fun just a little bit at the question.

Ali laughed good-naturedly. "Seriously. Tell me what you felt in there."

"I felt a little puzzled. The leaders seem to—I don't know what else to call it but love—they seem to love their students. And yet this isn't a soft love. They mean business!"

"Strictly speaking, 'puzzled' isn't a feeling," Ali chided, his face kind. "But I'm going to accept your answer. You felt the love. You saw the toughness. And your mind is puzzling over the apparent contradiction of these things."

Okay, so Ali's going to play shrink, too. Fair enough. I'm not famous for trafficking in the realm of feelings. "You're right. I felt the love, and I'm a little confused about what I saw."

"Which means you're going to get it. It's great stuff, isn't it?" he added, grinning broadly at my look of uncertainty. "But we can't linger, my friend," Ali pressed on, patting me on the back. "I've got to get you to our second appointment. On the surface, this one's going to appear entirely different—it's arguably one of the most successful biotechnology companies in the country. On closer inspection, though, I think you'll find some of the next building blocks of the Serving Leader model fitting right into the picture you started to get here at Aslan."

In the car, I reviewed what I had learned so far. The Serving Leader's first order of business is to Upend the Pyramid. This task has two dimensions: the Serving Leader moves to the bottom of the pyramid and the Serving Leader concentrates on building up others. My dad's comment about paradoxes came back to mind, and I saw the paradoxes of upending the pyramid. I also had a feeling that my conversation with Harry about standards was also going to present a paradox.

I was reflecting on my last question to Harry—about serving and being tough—when Ali pulled into BioWorks.

ACTION: RAISE THE BAR

"**B**io Works is on everyone's list of hot companies," Ali began. I started a fresh section in my journal. "It's an innovative, high science organization committed to next-generation sustainable technologies. Over the years, it has focused on agriculture and energy, especially in the area of biofuels. The company's work with biomass conversion points the way to energy sources that are totally renewable, carbon neutral, *and* biodegradable."

Puzzled, I glanced over at Ali. I had no knowledge of this field and hadn't understood a word he had just said.

"No greenhouse gases," Ali explained. "No global warming. And no dependence on foreign oil. It's big!" he added with a grin, making sure I saw the size of the frontier BioWorks was exploring.

"What you're going to find *really* interesting, though, is the competitive edge BioWorks has gained in this new global market through its commitment to Serving Leadership."

Arriving at a series of low-slung buildings, we were greeted at the door by Stephen Cray, one of the CEOs I had met the day before.

"Hi, guys!" he said. "Glad to see you again, Mike. Come on into my office."

"Stephen," I said, "you already know that I'm on a bit of a mission to understand the elements of being an effective Serving Leader. I have to confess, though, that I don't know a lot about biotechnology."

"I'm still learning myself," he said, flashing an easy grin.

"Well," I retorted, a bit nonplussed, "Ali's description of your work suggests you're at least a really fast learner."

Stephen just laughed. He ushered us into his office, and his assistant provided us with our choice of bottled water or soda.

"What I'm interested in," I pressed on, once we were all seated and served, "is how your company understands and practices leadership."

Stephen laughed again. "I guess I'd have to say that I'm not really an expert on leadership, either. But let me tell you what we know.

"At BioWorks, we believe that the big key is selecting the right people to join the team, those with the right skills and values, those who embrace our purpose of creating energy and making a difference in our communities."

I was listening intently, the hint of a question beginning to form behind the crease lines of my forehead.

"We're extremely disciplined about selection because we operate at a very high standard here. Frankly, it's hard to get into this company. We assess our recruits against a number of key competencies and values that have proven to be predictive of success in our organization. We do exhaustive interviews with candidates to see how they line up against those competencies and values. We push candidates to describe their specific behaviors and accomplishments in each of these areas. If they score well across all of them, they make it through our first screen."

Stephen grinned again, clearly aware of the growing frown on my face and of how high a standard he was describing.

"After that," he continued, unfazed, "candidates are interviewed by the people they'll work with. The team takes this very seriously. The interview is low key, but they're looking for the intangibles, candidates' values and their ability to work on a team. We look to see if they can add something positive to the culture here. Finally, we do exhaustive checks of external references. Like I said, we're picky." He laughed again, disarming his tough message.

"Here's a quote I keep on my desk," he continued, handing me a plaque.

> With all of his political duties—holding together the entire civilian and military war effort—he spent half of his time on placing people, finding the right person for a particular job at a particular time.
>
> —Peter F. Drucker, commenting on General George C. Marshall

"I've got to ask you to hold up for a second, Stephen," I finally interjected, unable to hold back my question any longer. "Ali just had me over at Aslan Industries, and I was hearing the very same thing there that I'm hearing from you. It's paradoxical, isn't it," I pressed on, now quite animated, "for a Serving Leader to be so tough on selection and standards? It seems like a contradiction. Serving seems so soft and, well, loving. But all I heard from Harry Donohue at Aslan was a tough line—and now I'm hearing it again."

Stephen gave me an emphatic nod of complete comprehension. "I know what you're saying. And there's surely no question whose son you are. Your dad is always talking about the paradoxes of effective Serving Leadership.

"Consider the term *Serving Leadership*. Two apparently contradictory words used together to create something true."

He had me there, and we smiled at each other. I may as well get used to these puzzles. Although I've been an explainer for a long time, maybe some of the good stuff isn't so easy to explain.

"I'll put it to you plainly," Stephen went on. "In order to serve many people, the Serving Leader must first pick just a few other leaders to serve, people who can meet the Serving Leader standard. Think about it, a Serving Leader who wants to create a powerful churn of productivity needs a team that can put itself at the full service of others. These teams, in their own turn, will serve others by building *them* up, and the results will keep spiraling outward. It all starts with a Serving Leader who really raises the bar."

I grabbed my notebook and quickly jotted down Stephen's phrase, "Raise the Bar," and what he had just said.

To serve the many, you first serve the few.

"The model used by Jesus of Nazareth is instructive here," Stephen said. "He could have chosen from thousands of his eager followers, but he chose only twelve, spending the rest of his time relating to them, *serving* them, and preparing them to do the very same with others. And look at the multiplied results that today validate his methodology."

"Okay, I see that," I interrupted. My tone was more curt than I intended. The subject of religion makes me uncomfortable, though it wasn't my intent to be rude. Ali and Stephen glanced at each other, noting my discomfort.

"Tell me more about this business of serving and developing the team to create success," I said, deciding to just press on.

"Sure thing," Stephen responded, undaunted by my boorishness. "We've got a saying around here that 'activity is no substitute for results.' In an organization like this, there is always more to do than can be done. We need to make choices, and we don't reward people for the mere process of doing things."

"Can you give me an example?"

"Sure. Even though we're a high-tech company, we're very skeptical about new technology. It's possible to fall in love with all of the new tools in our business. No one gets credit here for playing with new toys. We push our researchers and managers to be sure that we use the technology to create results. Our technology vendors know that we're a tough sell. We're notoriously difficult. But they know if they sell something to us, they can use us as the best possible reference around the rest of the world. I want to get the *very best* tools to serve our people, not just *lots* of tools. We are relentless about this. Let me walk you into the labs."

We were guided into an exotic-looking lab. A seven-person team greeted us.

"Say hello to Mike Wilson, everybody," Stephen began. "Some of you know his father, Robert Wilson."

The greetings became instantly warmer. My association with Dad clearly improved my standing.

"Mike is researching leadership in technology companies like ours. Why don't you tell him a little bit about the way we do things."

"Nice to have you with us, Mike," said an attractive, white-coated woman sitting to my left. "My name's Anna Park. I'm one of our software engineers. We help with the computer modeling that is always part of our early experimentation. I've had the pleasure of spending a little time with your dad," she added warmly.

She had my full attention. Anna looked to be in her middle thirties. She had an inquisitive and bright face that transformed her reasonable beauty into absolute radiance. Her more intimate comment about my dad also put me in a zone, I must add. She likes my dad, and I was getting some of that positive reflection.

"Leadership is key," Anna continued, "but your dad helped us think about leadership in terms of achieving team results. We set high standards for performance and then constantly raise the bar for ourselves. We expect more and more all the time."

"Would you tell me about that?" I asked.

"Okay, we meet daily to talk about the kinds of results we've gotten through the day's experimentation and to work out how that might be a stepping-stone to an ultimate result."

"You do that every day?" I asked.

"Every day!" she responded emphatically. "And then at the end of each week we line up each of those daily results on a white board and see how they might be connected. We're also linked to four other virtual teams around the globe. One in the U.K., another in Boston, a third in downtown Philadelphia, and one in San Diego. We link them in on Internet 2 and talk about the results of their week as well. Quarterly, we look at our success at hitting our goals and then raise the bar for our next quarter."

"That is *cool!*" I exclaimed, a bit unprofessionally.

"Well, actually, it is," Anna agreed, smiling at me broadly. "It used to be half the year before we would see each other and compare notes. Now we talk weekly."

"Another question. Your 'raise the bar' comment reminds me: Stephen used the same concept before we came in here. He tells me this is a hard place to get into."

"That's right," Anna replied firmly. I saw several of her colleagues nodding their heads with evident pride.

"Well, listen, I'm a little curious. What about the other side of the coin? Do Serving Leaders like you also push people out?" Quick glances were exchanged among the members of the team.

"It's a serious subject," Anna continued more soberly. "Think of how a hockey team works. There have been great young players who cannot play in the professional league. They show great potential but just don't make it at the next level. If they stay, it's a huge pitfall that can lead to mediocre team results. At BioWorks, when the rare situation occurs in which a person underperforms, we go into heavy coaching mode. If performance doesn't improve over time, we help him or her get a position somewhere else. I know it sounds harsh, but it's a very important process, and we work to honor everyone involved."

"Thanks," I said, shaking my head. I was amazed at the thought of the self- and group reflection that must go on here.

Back in Ali's car, we reviewed the day. Ali said, "Let me hear what you learned from the two sites today."

"Well," I began, "I started out hearing all about serving others. On the napkin yesterday, you upended the pyramid. Dorothy exemplifies this by moving to the bottom of the pyramid and serving everyone in her organization."

"And?"

"And then Harry strolled in, and we came over here and met Stephen and Anna, and all I've been hearing since then is these high standards. I had written down Stephen's expression, 'Raise the Bar,' and then Anna used it, too."

"And what's that about?" Ali asked, smiling. I knew that he knew and that he was enjoying watching me get up to speed.

"It's about two things, I think," I answered, content to play the role of good student. "First, it's about being selective in choosing the leaders you're going to work with. And, second, it's about continually raising the expectations for performance.

First, it's about being selective in choosing the leaders you're going to work with. And, second, it's about continually raising the expectations for performance.

"I must admit," I plowed on, "that I was biased against a serving approach to leadership. I thought it would be soft. You'd just serve whoever shows up, like you're ladling soup for the homeless."

"A common misconception," Ali said, the barest curve of a satisfied smile playing at the corner of his mouth.

"But it's a paradox." I flipped open to my note on this. I read: "To serve the many, you first serve the few."

"Right! It's about the multiplication of excellence." I guess he was ready to stop playing Socrates. "To serve the many," he continued, now showing his enthusiasm fully, the Serving Leader has to choose a few to focus on first, but through those few, you see, the team, the business, and then the community are *all* served.

"There is an exponential effect caused by the way a leader selects. Serving Leaders *must* be choosy. They must make the hard choice of who to pour themselves into based on who can reproduce this powerful Serving Leader approach with others."

"Okay," I said, interrupting him again. "I'm set with the issue of selection. But would you explain how it is that raising performance expectations fits into being a Serving Leader? I can see how it's good for the company. You get better results. But how is it good for the people, especially for the people who are struggling?"

"Both of these organizations are all about the people!" Ali retorted.

"I know that," I replied, "and I could see on everyone's face that it's true. But I want to know *how* it works. Aslan is working with people who have really gotten some bad breaks, and Harry's over there putting the hammer on them. You told me that I would get my question answered about this when we got to BioWorks."

"So your question is?"

"How does being tough on people help them? It helps you get a better product, I can see, and it helps you build a better company. But how does it help the people?"

"It has to do with the way human beings are made," Ali began. "We try to live up to what others expect of us. That's true for the rich and the poor, people who have an easy life or a hard one. Expect little, and we live up to the expectation. Expect a lot, and we stretch and grow to meet the expectation."

Ali paused to look at me, his face serious.

"I know some people who've grown up with everything you could ever want. Everything, that is, except high expectations and parental toughness. It isn't pretty. And it's the same for kids who suffer privation. If there's no expectation and no toughness, it isn't pretty."

Ali and I just looked at each other. I'd seen it, too. I guess I was thinking that the poor should be treated a little more forgivingly. Maybe given a little more of a break.

"What kind of service is it," Ali asked, as though he was reading my mind, "to deny a person the challenge to become really terrific? What kind of love would go soft and let a person come to no good? The best way to reach down to someone is to give them a challenging reason to reach up."

I wrote it down.

The best reach-down is a challenging reach-up.

"So that's it," I said. "People are people. Whatever their condition, you get greatness out of people by expecting it. That's just the way it is, however kind or unkind that may seem." I was in a reflective mood.

"That's part of it, Mike," Ali replied. "But just a part. Let's save some for tomorrow, shall we? You'll see that Raising the Bar isn't all there is. There's more that a Serving Leader needs to do than Upend the Pyramid and Raise the Bar."

As we pulled back into my mom and dad's driveway, I said, "I'm coming to the conclusion that I won't learn about Serving Leadership through just watching. I think I have to *become* a Serving Leader if I want to understand what you guys are doing here. Do you think I can get more hands-on experience?"

Ali smiled. "Your dad was absolutely right about you. You're the man we've been looking for. You'll get your chance. I believe the right serving opportunity is closer than you realize.

"And, Mike," Ali added as I was getting out of the car. "I'm so pleased that you joined us."

You joined us. That's what Ali said, though I can't really say that I ever agreed to join them. I agreed to *study* them, yes! But as I sit here again tonight in my childhood bedroom, thumbing through old baseball cards and a forgotten coin collection, I know that he's right. I *have* joined them. In helping them find words for these accomplishments, I am beginning to want to make them a part of my own life.

I'm the man they've been looking for!

With this thought, I settled into the task of writing up a quick review and update of the paradoxes I have noted— I know my dad will ask me about this, so I want to be ready for him!

Upend the Pyramid
You qualify to be first by putting other people first.
You're in charge principally to charge up others.

Raise the Bar
To serve the many, you first serve the few.
The best reach-down is a challenging reach-up.

I decided to also update my drawing of the pyramid. These principles are beginning to connect and build upon one another. At the beginning, at the bottom of the model, the Serving Leader upends the pyramid, as Dorothy does, placing herself at the service of building up the team. But this work of building up cannot be achieved with softness.

As Harry and Stephen and Anna described it, people are built up when the bar of expectation is raised high and when the key leaders are carefully selected so that the Serving Leader's powerful actions are replicated throughout the organization.

These two actions strongly reinforce each other. The Serving Leader undergirds and supports the members of the team and also establishes a challenging standard for everyone to reach. In this way, the Serving Leader's support is not soft and the Serving Leader's high standards are not inhuman.

Here's my new picture:

Raise the Bar

Upend the Pyramid

Sitting in this memory-filled room where I once had been so young and hopeful, it feels right to dream of the potential for places like Aslan and for an idea of leadership that is more than top-down command and control. It was in this room that I once lived with a sense of life's possibilities. My hands were open, not clenched. Same with my heart.

But all of these ancient artifacts also remind me of the losses. On my desk sits a picture of me and my first mongrel dog. I could tell him anything—I could cry with him when I was a boy—and he just loved me. The day he was hit and killed on our street was my first taste of terrible pain. What did I do with all that pain?

A picture of me with my old gang of buddies reminds me of all the jockeying to be first that went on in our group. I was in. I was out. I wanted to be accepted. I pretended I didn't care. I would wake up on many of those distant summer days sure that the new day would be perfect. And often it wasn't. So much of the time, I felt plain lost.

Finally growing up didn't exactly fix the problem, either!

Now I'm facing Dad's death and hanging out with a group of near strangers, and yet I feel in some small way less lost. I feel more *found*. It doesn't figure. My fondest designs for my life are being torn away, and yet I'm feeling more at home and at peace. Another paradox.

While I'm noting stuff I can't explain, I may as well address this matter directly. Dad's gang is very spiritual. Like at BioWorks earlier in the day, I've tried to steer clear of their forays into this subject. I'm surprised because in all my business consultancy, I've never talked with any clients about things like this. I'm not opposed to it, and I think I'm even open to learn more here. I am very uncomfortable in this area, though.

Dad filled me in tonight about his condition. He had been losing steam for months but disregarded it. He was also losing weight and losing his appetite. Stubborn! When he finally listened to Mom and saw his doctor, they sent him immediately to Johns Hopkins. Wrong type of tumor for surgery—for what they call the 'Whipple procedure.' Too large a tumor. And very bad results from nodal biopsies. All told, he's got a worst-case scenario for what, under ideal circumstances, is a worst-case cancer diagnosis. The only debate now is about what to do for symptom relief.

I shudder to think of the ordeal he's already endured. Colonoscopies, upper endoscopies, abdominal ultrasounds, CAT scans, MRIs, fecal fat and blood work, and more. All for the reward of receiving totally appalling news.

And yet Dad seems at peace! Why is that?

ACTION: BLAZE THE TRAIL

Dad and Mom headed back to the hospital this morning to review results from yesterday's tests. He is resolved about not wanting any medical heroics that will add no real value to the time he has left. They are considering, however, a round of radiation to deal with an intestinal blockage caused by tumor growth—we know, now, why Dad has no appetite.

I feel I should postpone my schedule. As much as Dad wants me out in the streets, I feel I should be spending time with him. My head's filling up with facts, principles, and diagrams, but my heart needs—I don't know what my heart needs. Instruction? Engagement? If I'm learning anything, I'm learning that the Serving Leader model can't be understood through principles and diagrams alone.

I think my relationship with Dad is a key. I still feel terribly disconnected from him. This is troubling to me because Dad tells me that a Serving Leader focuses on a new kind of relationship. Well, I'd like to have some of this new kind of relationship taking place between us.

Today Will Turner and Martin Goldschmidt gave me the whole day. They're an unusual and wonderful pair. Former Mayor Turner is African American, a gray-bearded Christian, gracefully companionable, and dressed to the nines. Goldschmidt is Jewish, reserved in speech and manner, and frumpily academic. They love each other and respect each other highly. I could use more days with men like this!

Dad told me last night that they are key to the whole Serving Leader project and that I'd gain much from my time with them.

"When I retired from my position as mayor," Will said in the car, "my life and career hit a brick wall. I had reached the top, achieved the goal of a lifetime of effort, and I wasn't even halfway through my fifties.

"I didn't know what to do with my contacts, energy, and passion for my city," Will continued. "I wasn't mayor anymore, but I still loved this city, and serving her had become the purpose of my life. I was in that stage of life one writer calls 'halftime.' I had success for myself, and I had served my city well, I believe. But I knew there was something even more significant that I was yet to do with my life."

"In my own very small way, I'm starting to understand what you're talking about," I said. "Not that I've achieved anything like you have," I quickly added, feeling a little dumb for making the comparison. "What I mean is, I'm not sure my goals will bring me the satisfaction I'm really looking for."

"You've just told me something very wonderful about yourself. You're on a venture, a journey toward your life's significance. I like that!"

I smiled dubiously. I *hope* that's true. I really do hope it!

"But tell me what the two of you are up to. All I know is that you're leading a nonprofit organization and that your work has strong coaching, mentoring, and teaching components."

"Will's doing all the work," Martin said. "I just watch in awe."

"Don't listen to that nonsense, Mike!" Will retorted. "Martin's research makes our work possible. Old do-gooders like me are notoriously soft on results, and that's unacceptable. Martin finds out if our good deeds actually do anybody any good. I need the validation he provides because life is too short to waste it on sentimental pursuits that don't actually improve anything. We want to move the needle on real social indicators in the community.

"What we're putting together here," Will continued, "is a teaching and mentoring program that's aimed specifically at children who have a parent in prison. Children of prisoners are among the most vulnerable populations in the city. Serving these kids yields incredible benefits for all of us. So we're building Serving Leaders who can work effectively with these kids. It is our focus on building leaders that gives us real hope for success here.

"We've activated churches and businesses throughout the city, working through Philadelphia's Big Brothers/Big Sisters organizations to coach these children. Your dad and Ali have been instrumental in helping us get started. Our Serving Leaders teach them reading, math, study skills, and, more importantly, life skills. All the while, they stick to them through thick and thin, hang out with them, give them a real relationship with an adult who's totally on their side.

"The point of it is," Will added, looking at me very firmly, almost challengingly, "these kids are getting loved!"

I just nodded my head. There isn't a professional category for it, but I'm starting to get the fact that love is part of the equation. Will's face told me I had met his challenge.

"These children are remarkable in their strength of will and ability to adapt. I'm very proud of what is happening to them." The expression on Will's face made that pride obvious.

Will and Martin took me to Big Brothers to see a mentor-training class. What an incredible cross section of Serving Leaders sat there: African American grandfathers, young suburban housewives, a Hispanic attorney on a break from work, a Vietnamese pastor, a couple of Philadelphia cops, as well as Muslims, Navy guys, Christians, Jews, and twenty-something Generation X-ers.

The trainer created several role-plays by bringing up different mentors to act out the scenarios that had been scripted. I was given a copy of the training manual and followed along as the group focused on a section called "Winning the Right." The role-plays focused on the initial encounter between a new mentor and a child, showing different ways that kids might resist someone who purports to care.

"These kids have lived through a lot of broken promises, ladies and gentlemen," the trainer said. "You're going to sound like one more promise that's just going to be broken, and your assigned child has had too much hurt already." The trainer spoke with the kind of authority that comes from having been there herself. "You've got to really understand that," she continued. "Don't misunderstand their bluff or their hardness. They might even do things just to make you angry. It's a test. Will you leave, too? Are you going to dismiss them as unredeemable like everybody else? They're going to test you, and I just want you to know something that's very, very important."

The teacher paused, piercing the class with her life-tempered, soul-rich eyes. No one stirred.

"The child you will be assigned desperately wants you to pass the test!" she concluded. Tears almost jumped out of my eyes. I understand being a kid and wanting a grown-up to pass the test. I didn't expect this visit to hit so close to home.

At the end of the class, the teacher asked Will Turner to say a few words. He tried to demur, but the teacher wouldn't have any of it. The former mayor dedicated his remarks to the task of affirming each of the men and women in the room for the "world-changing impact" each was making.

The mentors watched with keen attention as Will spoke, rapt with the words of appreciation they were hearing. This movement has tapped into something very profound, not only for the children that receive the help, but also for the people who are here to give of themselves. Will affirmed the difference these people are making in each other's lives, and he envisioned a community that would be healthier for their efforts. I pictured a "waterfall of service" cascading down from this team, bringing life to many.

After the class, Will and Martin took me to Will's office, housed in a Baptist seminary in West Philadelphia. Will started the discussion.

"The churches and businesses working together have been a key to our success here. Strong support has come from churches that have shifted from just taking care of themselves to equipping themselves for service in the community and then actually getting out there!"

"Do Baptists drink coffee, Will?" I asked, needing some reinforcement before we plowed on.

"Indeed we do, Mike. There's a nice coffee shop in the commons. Shall we walk and talk?"

As we headed out, I said, "I need some help. The Serving Leaders you are training to mentor kids are terrific. But I work in the corporate world. How does what these leaders do apply in business or in your former world of government? *Does* it apply?"

"Great question, Mike," Will answered approvingly. "We think that effective leadership, what we are calling Serving Leadership, is a key to creating lasting results. I've known this intuitively for many years, but it was Martin who helped clarify my thinking."

We filled coffee cups in the commons and took seats around a table by the tall, bright windows facing south from the campus.

"I believe the responsibility of any leader is twofold," Will continued. "We teach others the knowledge, skills, and strategies they need to succeed. And we work hard to get obstacles out of their way so they can make progress. In the inner city, our leaders teach the kids how to succeed while removing their barriers."

> We teach others the knowledge, skills, and strategies they need to succeed. And we work hard to get obstacles out of their way so they can make progress.

"Can you give me any examples of barriers?" I asked.

"Lots of them. A teacher at school who expects the child to fail—that's a barrier. You talk to that teacher and challenge him or her to see the child differently. And you keep at it so the teacher pays better attention. Or no healthcare is available when the child is sick—that's a big barrier. You take the mother or grandmother or whoever is raising the child to get a health card provided by the state. When the nine-year-old girl gets an earache, she also gets an antibiotic and some pain relief. And a lot of these kids can go to college, but they don't know that they can. That's a barrier. They'll never get there if you don't tell them it's possible, and then after you've told them, you walk them step by step the whole way through the process.

"So, it's a step at a time," Will continued. "Teach and remove barriers. And the very same principles apply in business or government. Serving Leaders have to reduce their wisdom on 'how to succeed' into bite-sized packages. The Serving Leader teaches these packages of wisdom to the team, which in turn teaches others."

"It sounds like what Noel Tichy has been saying for years," I interjected.

"Thanks to Martin, here, I actually know who you're talking about," Will said, smiling toward his silent sidekick. "He has made sure that I read *everything* pertinent to this subject."

Martin raised one eyebrow in restrained acknowledgment. I was becoming very curious about Dr. Goldschmidt. He hadn't said much so far, and yet I knew his hand was in everything I was seeing and hearing about.

"We find, though," Will continued, seemingly oblivious to my growing curiosity about this Penn and Teller routine, "that leaders often need training to become articulate about the 'how to succeed' wisdom that uniquely works in that organization."

Another acknowledging eyebrow from Goldschmidt. Apparently he thought his student, the former mayor, had done his homework well!

"The two of us are giving workshops to corporate and government executives on the 'teaching' and 'obstacle removing' practices of Serving Leaders. We call this area of our work 'Trailblazing' since a Serving Leader must both teach and remove obstacles so that others can follow the path they've blazed.

"It's trailblazing in another way," Will added, a playful smile on his face. "We're blazing a trail right into the heart of your consulting business!"

I had this whole thing wrong! I'd figured them for sophisticated do-gooders. But then I started hearing about the high standards—at BioWorks, the theme was "Raise the Bar." And now I'm listening to a man who's using the Serving Leader approach to outcompete me with corporate executives. Charlie was right. This is a new game!

"Mind telling me your approach with corporate executives?" I asked. "You don't want to leave me back in the dust, do you?"

"Room up front for all of us, Mike," Will responded kindly. "Our approach is simple. We help executives become better teachers. They become more articulate about the strategies, tactics, models, tools, and approaches that uniquely work in their own corporations. These leaders are the first teachers, their students in turn becoming the next set of faculty, and so forth, down through the organization. We design it so that one group serves the next, passing along knowledge relevant to the most pressing problems faced in the organization."

"I have an image of a teaching waterfall," I said, "with the impact cascading throughout the organization."

"That's a wonderful picture," Will responded, his face filled with warmth.

"But is there any danger of working yourself out of a job doing what you say?" I continued. "If you teach everything that you know, then maybe *you're* not needed anymore."

Will's face brightened, his eyes now twinkling with good humor. "It's a paradox," he declared. "Ever hear of a paradox?"

I just laughed.

"The more you teach your people to not need you, the greater your value," he pressed on. "Want to hang onto your value? Give everything you have away." Now his face was positively radiant. I grabbed my pen.

To protect your value, you must give it all away.

"But hold on," he continued. "We're not finished with the point—there's another step. Remember your image of a waterfall? The second step is to remove the boulders and obstacles in the current that impedes the flow. Teaching and removing obstacles need to go together. We teach this in our workshops. But may I share a few words yet about the additional *process* we use to build Serving Leaders?"

"Please!" I almost shouted. My hand was cramped from writing, but I knew I'd hit a mother lode, and I wasn't going to stop digging now!

"We lay out the model of Serving Leadership, with readings, tutorials, and exercises. Frankly, I use the life and teachings of Jesus as one of the models here."

My turn to raise a Goldschmidt-ian eyebrow. A quick glance at Martin told me we would have scored well on synchronization just then.

"Outside the workshops, we implement what we call 'walking the talk.' On a regular schedule, we observe our leaders at work, collect feedback from their colleagues, and then give the leaders direct feedback on how their behavior compares to the behavior of a Serving Leader. This can be painful.

"And finally," Will concluded, "we encourage these men and women to join or create what we call an 'encouragement group' of trusted colleagues who help each other persevere in pursuit of their leadership and personal goals."

"And by the way," Goldschmidt interjected, startling me with this sudden foray into the conversation, "we only teach leaders who have *really* joined us. We take clients who are committed to developing as Serving Leaders. No half-hearted students make our cut."

I heard Martin's last comment and felt a chill. They were practicing strategic selection, just like Stephen Cray at BioWorks. This "loose" team of people isn't loose at all. They are building on each other's learning and using each other's principles. There is an integration here, and I know now that my dad is up to something incredible.

I felt a chill for another reason. Martin said they only take clients who really join them. And Ali thanked me yesterday for joining them. And hadn't I said I wanted my research to become more hands-on? This wasn't just another assignment; it was becoming much more personal than that.

"Mike, I'm afraid you're going to have to hold any other questions," Will added. "Our time's up—I tutor a thirteen-year-old boy in half an hour and must go pick him up." Answering the question on my face, he said, "Yes. I walk the talk!" Will's smile was proud and resolute.

"Martin will take you back. Let me give you an outline we use to describe our Trailblazing model."

I thanked Dr. Turner, took his outline, and headed out with Martin.

In the car, Martin and I spoke for a few minutes about his relationship with the former mayor. He then asked me to look over the outline Will had just handed me.

1. Serving Leaders build teaching organizations to create excellence at every level.
2. Leaders who teach become consistent in their own performance—leaders learn to introspect, to articulate their knowledge, and to improve consistency.
3. Serving Leaders remove obstacles so others can succeed.

"I asked you to read that, Mike," Martin said when I'd finished, "because I want to add a very important point. Maybe the most important one.

"I'm not in this business to make organizations work better; I should just declare that outright. Lots of organizations work well enough but add nothing to the world.

"I want to see communities being restored, lives improving, kids learning to read, prostitutes breaking the drug and economic chains that hold them, neighborhoods gaining local jobs. That's what I'm after."

I was listening very quietly, aware that Martin was speaking from a depth of passion. After he spent the morning in near silence, I suspected that his spare remarks would be worth waiting for.

"There's some powerful research my team at the university has been working on for several years. I won't bore you with the details of methodology and statistics, but the implications are clear."

My pen was poised.

"Simple fact: if you want to do something that really changes someone's life, the best thing you can do is make the person you're trying to help a participant in the process. If all you have are passive clients—or employees or students or parishioners for that matter—you've got nothing."

I looked at him quizzically, waiting for the connection.

"The research is clear. When the working poor are enlisted to help build houses for themselves and others, they become responsible homeowners. When a prostitute going through recovery and life-skills training is put on the team that assures that other prostitutes receive training, that woman doesn't slide back into a life of prostitution. When neighbors who need their block rid of pushers are given the opportunity and the know-how to join the police to get rid of the pushers, the block stays clean. Simple fact, Mike, well researched."

"Why is that?" I asked, my spine tingling with a sense of the great significance in his remarks.

"Because substandard housing, prostitution, illiteracy, and drugs are not the core problem," Martin replied hotly. "The fact that human beings have no sense of belonging to a real *community* is the problem. And what is that sense of belonging to a real community all about?"

I waited.

"The experience of community is when we know that we're important to the team! Everyone's in the game. Leaders put others first. Leaders expect great things from everybody. Leaders teach and get rid of obstacles for others.

Community happens when *everyone* rolls up their sleeves and gets to work.

"Giving our clients services doesn't make community," he continued. "Neither does just giving them training.

Community happens when *everyone* rolls up their sleeves and gets to work. Only a Serving Leader can catalyze that kind of a miracle!"

I have to say it. This was an incredible day. I'm going to be considering these remarks for a very long time. What I'm really hoping for is the chance to *see* and *experience* what Will and Martin talked about today. I want to become a part of the kind of community experience they described.

When I got home, I visited with my folks until they went to bed. I began to collect my notes for the day and had just updated my pyramid when Ali stopped by. He wanted to hear about my day so we moved out to the porch to talk. Ali was back to his teacher's role—which, all gibes aside, I really appreciate.

"Summarize for me," he said, after I had told him about the day. "What's been added to your picture?"

"All of these Serving Leaders are outstanding teachers," I began. "They give their followers very specific advice on what to do and how to do it, based on their own success using these same approaches. Their teaching has credibility because they live what they teach. Will's expression is 'Walk the Talk.'"

"That's good," Ali said. "But is it sufficient to teach people what to do and then to stand back and hope they succeed?"

I pulled out my updated pyramid—graduated from a napkin to a proper journal entry—and told him about Will's use of the term "Trailblazing."

"Trailblazers do more than teach," I continued. "They push obstacles out of the way of the people they are serving." This was really starting to click, to come together, to make sense to me. "They are obliterating red tape," I continued. I was on a roll. "They are deep-sixing all the non-

Blaze the Trail

Raise the Bar

Upend the Pyramid

sense policies and sweeping away all the barriers that keep people from success. Their success lies in clearing the path for others to succeed." (Yes, I noted the paradox—and added it to my growing list!)

"The Serving Leader is a trailblazer," I concluded, now fully feeling my rhythm. "All levels of leadership in an organization trailblaze for their teams, teaching and removing obstacles, and the team members then do it for their own teams. Bang! Now we've got enough clear running room for a whole company to really acceleratate down the track!"

Ali liked it. He took another forty-five minutes to tell me how much he liked it and—I guess I'll just say it—to really pour on the affirmation. If my mother had been awake to hear it, she'd have warned me about getting a swelled head. No danger. It's my heart that's swelling.

After Ali left the house, the hour quite late, I thought again of that great picture of my dad making his own sprint down the track. That set me thinking.

There's a painful irony about my dad's leadership. He is truly the expert in Serving Leadership. And yet, his son doesn't feel that he ever got much benefit from it.

I always thought my dad had set an unreachable leadership standard. I didn't know how to reach it, that's for sure. And if I couldn't reach his standard, then I'd never be able to reach him. I may as well have been a welfare client staring across the uncrossable gulf between myself and the well-dressed professional looking over my claim. That's the feeling—I could never hope to reach his standard. I could never hope to be like him. At the deepest level, I could never hope. So why even bother trying?

But the truth is, my dad is far from perfect, and I'm sure he knows it acutely, probably painfully.

So he's not perfect, yet look at all the incredible goodness he's unleashed.

In the past, I felt terribly angry about this. There was no hope that Dad would ever really be in my corner—I would never be able to do enough to win his favor—and all the while he was always in everyone else's corner! He was out there blazing trails for *other* people, removing *their* obstacles, never doing it for me. Honestly, he wasn't even around enough to know what my obstacles were.

So how do I feel about this now? Now I feel, well, hopeful. Just hopeful. How about that. My father's not perfect, and yet he's done such great good. And I'm not perfect, either. So maybe, like father, like son.

Dad has opted for radiation. I bagged my plans for a while. Time to be with Dad. I told Ali I was going to look for some hands-on experience, didn't I? So where exactly was I planning to look?

MENDING A BROKEN TRACK

Charlie called me today, wondering how my project's coming along. He's been checking in with Dad every few days and knew full well that my project has not been coming along. That is, not my Philadelphia project.

As to the deeper project, the project of myself and my dad, so much has taken place.

For three weeks now, I've been spending time with Dad and Mom. His radiation treatments ended today. Three weeks of daily trips to U. Penn., new pictures each day, followed by an hour of setup—all in preparation for each day's mere seconds of radiation. The pictures look better. The blockage is open. But, frankly, Dad's only weaker. He is eating more, and Mom and I are glad about that.

I guess I was not really surprised to hear from Charlie. As much as he understands the fact that I'm going through a difficult time with my dad, he really doesn't understand. He's my boss, and he expects me to show him something for all this time. I think he's losing his patience. I understand more now about Charlie's sense of indebtedness to my dad. Dad asked him to do this so he's doing it. But I sense the day is coming very soon when Charlie will have had enough. So be it!

What I *have* been surprised about is how often I've heard from so many others, especially my new friends here in Philly. *New* friends! Makes it sound like I had a bunch of old ones, which I'm realizing now that I really didn't.

Dr. Turner has stopped in to see Dad and me almost every day. Ali's stopped by several times and phoned frequently. Dad and I have both gotten cards and notes, and Stephen Cray sent flowers. Even Martin and Dorothy have both stopped by, to my great surprise. And most interestingly, Anna Park has called me a few times to ask how I'm doing. Her calls have meant a lot to me, these gestures of kindness so clearly not required of her.

And *none* of them have asked about my research. They just wanted to offer comfort and kindness to me. It makes me cry to think about it, something, candidly, that I've been doing a lot lately.

So my journal's been totally neglected for three weeks. In fact, I'm no longer sure of its value for anyone but me. It has become very personal—too personal, I think, to serve the purpose Charlie first had in mind.

Before any more time passes, I want to try to capture what's been going on between Dad and me—what's been occupying my days and nights over these weeks.

For the first couple of days with Dad, between going with him for his treatments and trying to help him and Mom at home, I tried to use part of my time to organize my notes. I'd collected a lot of material that I needed to think through, but it was just not coming together for me. I finally decided to let it alone. So I pushed myself more into taking care of Dad. It was very uncomfortable for both of us at first. We are not used to spending that kind of time together, and Dad was clearly embarrassed about how weak and dependent he had become. It must be especially difficult for him, given his lifelong role as the man in charge, the man on top.

My own discomfort shames me. I've spent a lifetime wanting to be closer to my dad, but the truth is that being close to him does not come easy for me. More truth: I don't think I've ever been good at being close to anyone. When Susan left me ten years ago, I didn't understand what her problem was. And I thought it was her problem. For the first time since that awful experience, I doubt that it was her problem. "I just feel I can't get close to you" is what she kept saying. And I dismissed it. This hurts and shames me deeply; she wanted to be close to me.

In the here and now, though, I'm also feeling proud of myself. Discomfort or no, I have pushed myself to help provide for Dad's physical care, and I've begun to feel a deepening satisfaction from it. I help him walk, feed him when he can eat, and keep his room clean. Lately, I've started helping him to shave. I feel useful to him, and it feels good. After these many days so close together, we have begun to really talk. And, as I said already, I've begun to cry, sometimes a lot, often when I'm back in my room after spending the day with Dad. Deep feelings have been coming to the surface for me that I have not allowed myself to feel for a very long time.

One morning last week, Dad and I launched into a long and winding discussion about the years of my growing up. Soon we had every family album open on his bed. It was wonderful. Outside it was raining so hard that at times the thrumming of rain on our roof sounded like a waterfall. Another waterfall of goodness.

"Remember when we had that old Volkswagen camper and you welded an extra bed into it so I could take a friend along on our trips?"

"Sure I remember it, Mike."

"One of my best memories growing up was when you and I would go out and sleep overnight in the VW, just in our driveway." Dad's eyes misted, a deeply grateful smile on his face. "Those were such good times. We'd really talk. It feels a lot like that now," I added.

"I'm so glad you came home, Son," Dad answered. "I'm glad we have this time together to talk again."

"A little later, when you're feeling better, I'd like to go through all these pictures of you and Mom and have you tell me the stories of what was going on in your life during those times. I'd like to put a little note on the back of each of these pictures."

"That's a good idea," Dad said, sounding a little doubtful. "But didn't you say that later is going to have to be sooner? I'm thinking it's going to need to be real soon."

I glanced up and caught Dad's eye. We just looked at each other for a long moment.

"Mike," he continued, clearing his throat. "I have to ask you a question that's been on my mind for many years." He paused again before continuing. "What are your memories and feelings from your growing-up years here in Philly?"

"Well," I stammered, needing to decide how to answer him. "They're mostly happy, Dad," I offered tentatively.

"But there was sadness, too, wasn't there?"

I nodded.

"I wish so much that we had taken more times like this, Mike. Times together. I didn't give you what a son needs from his father."

"I was always proud of you," I protested. "You were definitely my hero growing up. You always bought me neat toys," I added lamely. I sat still for a moment, considering whether to say what I was really feeling. I decided it was now or never. "To be honest, though," I said more slowly, less certainly, "I would have preferred just to have more of you."

Dad was still for a moment, absorbing my comment.

"I deserve that," he said with a heavy sigh, his chin slumping a little bit more into his chest. "I've really needed to talk about this with you." He reached over and touched my arm to make his point, looking up at me. "I've got real regrets, Mike. I haven't been a perfect dad. Not even close. I think, in part, I bought you those things to try to assuage my guilt over our lack of time together. I could tell when you were going through struggles, and I guess I hoped your mother would take care of those things. I tried to give you advice—to be your coach—but I wasn't much of a listener. I guess I delegated my work as a father to your mom, and I know now that it doesn't work that way.

"Do you remember the Michael stories I used to tell you?" Dad asked hopefully.

"Sure, I remember them. You used to start them with 'Once upon a time, there was a boy named Mike,' and then you'd tell a story about how to stay away from strangers or how to watch out for myself. I loved those stories!"

"Well, I guess that was my attempt to give you fatherly advice. But I never really talked with you about what was going on. I regret that so much. The real reason I wanted you to come home to work with me on these projects was so you and I could talk about this. I have something important to ask you." Dad straightened himself up in his bed.

I sat very still, waiting, not knowing, what I was about to hear.

"Will you forgive me for all those times I wasn't there for you?" Dad's eyes were brimming over with tears, his face filled with grief.

"Oh, Dad," I almost wailed. "Of course I forgive you. You've been terrific!"

"No, please, don't sugarcoat it! I haven't been!"

I wasn't sugarcoating it. Yes, I'd felt abandoned as a child. But all I could feel in this moment was that my dad had been terrific. That I was terrifically lucky to have him as my dad. To still have him.

I put my arms around him, and for a long moment we squeezed each other hard, both our shirts damp from the other's tears.

"You haven't lost *all* your strength," I offered playfully. "You about broke my back."

He just snorted, grateful, I think, for the lightened mood. By the look on his face, though, he was clearly not finished with all he wanted to say.

"I really am proud of you, Dad." I pressed on. "I was proud of your career, and I'm even prouder of what you're doing now. I think you're making a real difference here in the city, and it means the world to me that you wanted to bring me into it."

Dad responded slowly, "That's the other thing I wanted to talk to you about. I *do* feel good about the difference we're making with Serving Leadership here. But on the other hand, I feel a terrible heaviness about it."

I was confused and must have done a good job of showing it on my face.

"Not about the work in the city," he quickly explained. "My heaviness comes from seeing how wide the gulf is between my public life and my family life."

Now I got it, and I never loved my dad more.

"I tout Serving Leadership, and I never really served you and your mom! Not really. I'd march out there onto the grand stage representing all those virtues, and all the while I was missing the boat so badly where it mattered most. The more I work to serve others in the community, the more I can't think of anything else except all those soccer games I missed or the train set we never finished in the basement or the hundreds of other things I don't even know about. I've felt like such a hypocrite." He finished imploringly, his voice almost a whisper now.

A lifetime of misunderstanding rearranged itself in my heart in that moment. Dad had always been proud of me. Dad had always wanted to be with me. All those times that I wasn't able to get his approval, those times I'd look over at him hoping to catch his approving eye, his glances away weren't because he was ashamed of his son; they were because he was ashamed of *himself*. All I can say is "Wow!" My dad has struggled with many of the very same things I've always struggled with.

"Look at me, Dad," I said, surprised at my assertiveness. Dad's confession made me feel like a man, not like a lost and hopeless boy. "I forgive you," I said emphatically, lovingly. "I assure you that you don't need it, because I absolutely hold no blame in my heart toward you. But I want you to know it clearly. I totally forgive you!"

My dad looked at me with peace and satisfaction shining from his eyes. He took a deep breath, a good breath, and just kept looking at me.

"Thank you, Son," he said simply.

I can't express how good it felt to have him look at me the way he did—and speak to me the way he did. Like he was pleased with me.

I took my own deep breath, took in what I was being given, and prepared myself.

"I've got a confession, too."

Dad wasn't slumped over anymore. His gaze was level, his kind eyes welcoming whatever it was that I needed to say.

"Some of those nice things that you and Mom bought for me, I not only didn't appreciate, I set out to destroy them. I had the neatest new wagon in the neighborhood, but I popped the wheels off to ruin it."

Dad smiled. He seemed glad for the truth.

"I found those wheels and what was left of the wagon, too. I never did understand what had happened."

"There were feelings behind what I did, Dad."

He nodded. Of course there were.

"And that great train set you got for me that seemed to cover the world. When I was angry with you, I'd start breaking it apart. I loved that train set, but what I really loved was our time working on it together. When you weren't around, I'd go down to the basement and take out my anger on those trains. I was angry with you and I never told you. I wasn't ever really fair with you. I just kept my feelings hidden.

"I've broken other things, too," I plowed on, needing to get it all out on the table. "I've never been exactly open about my feelings as an adult, either. And I never asked you for help when I needed it. I know that you and Mom were terribly disappointed about what happened to my marriage, but I just kept you away.

"I felt like I was just a failure—that there was a stigma attached to me. That's when I stopped going to church. I didn't belong there. I didn't feel like I belonged anywhere, to tell you the truth." Now it was my turn to cry.

"I'm so sorry, Mike."

"Hey, it's supposed to be my turn to say that I'm sorry," I blurted out, laughing through my tears. "And I am sorry, Dad."

"Mike, our hearts were broken when you struggled in your marriage. We love you so much and only wanted to stand by your side. The church only wanted that, too. None of us are perfect."

Dad and I talked a long time that night about hurt feelings and missed opportunities. This was a huge breakthrough for me. I started to realize how I'd managed my life in order to protect myself from the hurt, how I'd pushed people away, not letting them get too close where they could hurt me. Being with my dad that night—seeing both of us in a new light—allowed me to see how I needed to heal my relationships with others.

Later that night, after Dad had gone to bed, I started the first of a series of phone calls seeking forgiveness from people I've walked away from, that I've hurt or offended or lied to. My first call was to Susan. She sounded really apprehensive, and then she understood what I was doing. We cried and laughed, and she told me how happy she is, how much she loves her children, that it's a good marriage. I wished her all the best, and I meant it. She wished me well, too. I hung up with a great pain in my heart. And a great release.

I made other calls that night, and I was so surprised and grateful for the reactions I got. People were quick to forgive and happy to reset the clock in our relationship. A burden's being lifted from my heart.

During our morning cup of coffee, I shared these phone calls with my dad.

"Thank you, Dad. If you hadn't taken the step that you did to bring healing to our relationship, I wouldn't be doing this. I wouldn't know how." I gave him a moment to absorb this. Then I smiled. "So you've gone right ahead and brought all that goodness you've been sharing around Philadelphia right back into your home. That's Serving Leadership, Pop. At least if I've got the concept right."

Dad just shook his head. I really liked the way he was looking at me.

"You remember that train trip we took together?" he asked, changing the subject.

"I loved it," I exclaimed, "especially because it was an overnight trip, and we had that sleeper car. It's one of the times I remember that we really talked."

"Do you remember the plans we made while we looked out the window?"

"How we were going to build our own new train set in the basement," I answered, aware again of so much that we'd lost.

"Well, if you'll help me navigate the stairs, I've got something I want to show you." I opened the door and helped Dad down into the dark basement. There, laid out like a perfect little city, was a replica of my old electric train empire. It was like going back through a time warp. It looked perfect, like the days we had worked on it together.

"Dad, what's this? You got another one just like my old Lionel set?"

"Not at all, Mike," Dad beamed. "It's the original! I've been thinking about you and me getting reconnected now for several years. Shame on me that it took what it took for it to happen. But that's not important anymore, is it?"

I shook my head. It wasn't important.

"Well, I've spent quite a lot of time down here—not lately, of course—putting this set back together. I fixed the tracks, repaired some of the buildings, bought some parts, and rebuilt the whole thing. Mending this old train night after night helped me think through the mending we needed to do. There's still a bit more to do before we can turn the power back on, and I *had* hoped that we could do it together."

"I'll finish what you started, Dad," I said. "You can count me in!"

ACTION: BUILD ON STRENGTH

Another week has passed since I made my last notes. Dad has enjoyed a real bounce in both energy and appetite, and he's bent on putting both himself and me back into play in our Serving Leader project. Mom, Dad, and I all know that this bounce is only temporary, that, in fact, it might be very short-lived. We want to make the most of it.

Yesterday I reviewed with him the work I've done so far, showed him my journal, and talked at length about what I've been learning. I watched him intently while he read— saw his smiles, his nods, and at times his outright laughter. And I was riveted to his face for a couple of incredible moments when he stopped his reading, tears in his eyes, to look up at me.

"This is really good," he said simply when he had finished. His face told me everything a son wants to know.

We talked about how personal my journal has become, and Dad told me this was, in his estimate, the best part of it.

"If it wasn't personal, Mike," he declared, "it wouldn't be worth a thing!"

His strong statement startled me. He made his point.

"You wrote what Martin had to say about helping people," Dad explained. "I've found that his point applies to everybody, children of prisoners and CEOs alike. If all we're doing is offering services or insights to people, we're just playing that tired old dependency game. *All* of us must make our contribution. It *has* to be personal. *All* of us must bear the fruit of this work in our own lives.

"We're on the same team now," he added with a smile. "This journal weaves it all together, yourself included. Nothing could please me more."

Nothing could please me more, either. I'm on my dad's team!

"But you're not done," Dad said matter-of-factly. "Some important dimensions are still not woven into the story."

I waited while he collected his thoughts.

"All the partners we've involved, Mike—the police, the corporate executives, the pastors—have to be connected to each other because they each bring a strength to the table that is needed by others. Isolated greatness, whether it's in the police department, a profitable business, or a growing church, isn't greatness at all. We need our *communities* to come back to life. We're doing this work in order to make the kind of citywide impact that can only be made when we bring our collective strengths to the service of the whole."

Dad paged back to my pyramid diagrams and reviewed my terms: Upend the Pyramid, Raise the bar, Blaze the Trail.

"I need you to look at some great work done in Chicago several years ago by John Kretzmann and John McKnight.

Martin has spent a lot of time with these guys looking at how you build on the strengths of a community."

He pulled their workbook down from his shelf, and we spent an hour paging through it as Dad explained how the Serving Leader paradigm encompasses the larger community.

"Here's another paradox for you," he then said. "You've heard that the best way to improve yourself is to work on your weaknesses. It turns out that the opposite is true."

I frowned in puzzlement. I've been working on my weaknesses for decades. Well, okay, so maybe these efforts haven't been all that effective.

"Paradoxically," Dad continued, "you get better results by shifting attention away from your weaknesses. It's far more productive to shift your focus to your strengths."

"Sounds irresponsible," I said, deadpan. Actually, giving it a moment's thought, it sounded pretty good. Still, it didn't sound quite proper.

"The Serving Leader's job is to focus everyone on the team and in the organization and in the community on living out their strengths. When people are living out their day-to-day lives by exercising their strengths, they're more productive and, frankly, happier."

"Okay," I drawled. "So you just pretend you don't have any weaknesses?" Isn't that what I've always done? Hasn't that been precisely the thing that's gotten me into trouble?

"Pretend you don't have weaknesses?" Dad laughed. "And who'd buy that? No, Mike. The point is that it's dumb to pour all your good life energy into turning weaknesses into serviceable mediocrity!"

All right, so this is starting to make sense.

"The better approach is to bring together a team where the individual strengths offset the individual weaknesses. A high-performance team is put together with the greatest

care and attention to how each person's strengths can be used to the max
and how the weaknesses will get covered by someone else on the team.

"In my first corporate lead role,"
Dad continued, "I figured out that I
was terrible administratively. My in-
stincts were scarily accurate when it
came to spotting a new opportunity
for our company and then in knowing
what would be needed to translate
that opportunity into success. But I'm not good when it
comes to the follow-through. Once I saw the opportunity
and conceived a strategy to implement it, I stopped paying
the kind of attention that's needed. So I made sure I had a
COO that was gifted administratively. Together, we were
quite a team. I helped craft high-level strategy, and my COO
made sure things got translated administratively into tactical
plans with *i*'s dotted and *t*'s crossed.

"Serving Leaders must work to create teams where everyone is living out their strengths day to day. This applies
to small teams, to midsized organizations, and to whole
communities.

"Now here's my point," Dad concluded. "In the same
way that good Serving Leaders in a corporation build upon
the strengths of their employees, Serving Leaders in a community build upon the assets that are already present there.
They don't put their focus on the problems but rather on
the solutions that already exist.

"I'm calling the No-Name Team to a special meeting,"
he declared suddenly, as though he'd just made up his mind.
"I don't have much time, and I don't care if there are stock-
holder meetings or black-tie dinners at the White House.

> A high-performance
> team is put together
> with the greatest care
> and attention to how
> each person's strengths
> can be used to the
> max and how the
> weaknesses will get
> covered by someone
> else on the team.

We're meeting tomorrow! This work is more important than anything any of them might have on their calendars."

I just smiled. Dad was feeling like the boss again, and I loved seeing him like this. I also sensed that he was preparing himself for a final push to the finish line.

I made note of Dad's point:

To address your weaknesses, focus on your strengths.

We met this morning, everyone convening in a section of the city Dad identified on the map as Greenwood. "Where're we going?" I asked as Dad directed me along the streets. I'd never visited Greenwood, never driven through it, and never met anybody from there, in fact. Indeed, there was nothing green about it. A more miserable twenty-five city blocks I have never seen.

"We're in the heart of our city's best hope," Dad answered evenly.

I must have had an incredulous look on my face because Dad just grabbed my arm. "You need new eyes. Eyes to see what's here, not what's not. Remember what we just talked about yesterday? Build on strength?"

I remembered, and I was looking. But I couldn't see!

"I'm going to introduce you to an old friend this morning, someone who will help to improve your eyesight."

We arrived in the parking lot of a well-weathered red-brick church. Our meeting took place in the church basement, this venue being quite a surprise to me, especially after starting out five weeks ago at the Pyramid Club.

We walked down the steps into the church's fellowship hall, and everyone was there, those I'd already met as well as nearly thirty others.

The chief of police came, along with his community liaison officer. Two hospital administrators were present, an editorial-page writer for the *Enquirer*, nearly a dozen neighborhood leaders and organizers, the mayor's chief of staff, several local pastors, Alistair Reynolds, Will Turner, Dorothy Hyde and Harry Donohue from Aslan, Stephen Cray and Anna Park from BioWorks, Martin Goldschmidt's university research team, and many other business leaders.

I don't think I've ever been in such a circle, certainly not in my consulting work. This group was as female as it was male, more African American than White, and also Hispanic and Asian. And the spirit was delightful; these people knew each other, and the banter told me that they also liked each other.

A large square of folding tables had been arranged for us, encircled by folding metal chairs. I was greeted by many of my new friends and introduced to many others. Dad was obviously the guest of honor. Everyone wanted to say a word to him, give him a hug and, in the case of many of the women in the circle, a kiss. I saw their looks of dismay and their exchanged glances of sorrow as they realized how much weight he had lost, how frail he looked. Dad was among his family, and the care they showed him was deeply moving to me.

We took our seats, and I was pleased that Anna positioned herself next to me.

"Ladies and gentlemen, can I call you all to order?" Dad's voice was clear but very weak. You could have heard a pin drop.

"Some of you have already met my son, Mike." Nods, smiles, and "Hey, Mikes" all around. "He's writing our story, and, fatherly bias aside, it's as good a piece of work as I've ever seen."

I felt a small blush crawl up around my ears and really liked seeing the smiles that showed the group's love for Dad. Somehow, I felt that their love for him was being graciously extended to cover me, as well. As to the compliment, I doubted anyone believed that "fatherly bias" had been set aside in the least.

"I think your father's wonderful," Anna whispered, leaning close. I started to slouch toward her to acknowledge her comment.

"Mike," Dad barked, "I called this meeting for you, so pay attention!"

Everyone roared at the start this gave me. They'd all been called to better order at one time or another by Dad's commanding instructions and clearly enjoyed seeing the old man's boy get the very same treatment. I was sitting very straight and tall now. Dad looked pleased with himself.

"Usually, quarterly meetings are devoted to our community-building projects," he continued. "The goal of the No-Name Team is to serve the communities of our city by developing stronger Serving Leaders throughout all city sectors. We support these leaders with many kinds of needed resources and then magnify their impact through the strategic interconnections of this broad group. Occasionally, we even help them find expert consulting services, I might add," he said, winking at me.

"Traditionally, the community sector is left out of the equation, Mike," Dad went on, now addressing me directly. "But we think of our work in the first three sectors—the public, the private, and the nonprofit—as all needing to contribute to the building of the most important fourth sector, the community. Our work, then, to put it simply, is to develop the Serving Leader model in each of these sectors—building their teams and organizations—and then to connect these sectors to improve the life and vitality of the communities and neighborhoods where people actually live."

By this time I was writing furiously.

"For our meeting today, I'd like to ask my friend Jim Silver to update us on developments underway right here in Greenwood. Jim?" he said, nodding to a man about my age seated across the table from us.

"Listen up, Son," Dad added, enjoying this final fatherly gibe.

"I'd like to just say, as an introduction, that Robert Wilson is a money grubber," Jim began, causing the group to again collapse into laughter. My dad was grinning broadly. "I've brought your lousy hundred bucks, Bob," Jim continued. "You thought I was going to try to weasel out of it, didn't you?"

I wondered what he was talking about.

"It was your dad, Mike," Jim continued, "who got me stuck in the middle of everything here. He and I met while flying back from a business convention, and we just started talking on the plane about the sad state of some of Philadelphia's urban communities. Anyway, he asked me if I thought I was really putting my best gifts to use for the broader community, and frankly, I knew that I wasn't. The fact of the matter is that I wasn't putting my best gifts to use for anything! I was at the very top of my game, head of the company, and feeling like an empty shell. I think your dad sensed it, Mike. He says to me, 'Jim, I've got a big idea that I'd like you to consider.'"

More chuckles. My dad has apparently buttonholed more than one person with one of his big ideas for their life.

"'I'd like you to do an experiment, Jim,' he told me. 'Do you believe in prayer?'"

"'*Of course*,' I said. Which was a total exaggeration, I'll tell you right now. What I knew about prayer was a joke."

Laughter gave way to serious listening.

"'Well, then I'd like you to pray every day for Greenwood,' Bob says. Greenwood! I thought. Why Greenwood? 'We'll put a bet on it,' he said, 'and six months from now, if something significant hasn't happened in Greenwood, I'll give you a hundred dollars.'"

"I told Bob then that I didn't blame him for only making it a hundred since I knew enough about Greenwood to not expect anything significant to ever happen here."

I noticed several of the attendees looking rather stoical at this remark. They were Greenwoodites, I surmised, and less than amused by Jim's negative press on their neighborhood.

"Well, I took Bob's challenge, and I took it seriously," Jim continued. "I started praying for Greenwood every day, but then I began to figure that I couldn't really pray for this neighborhood unless I knew a little bit more about it. So I got a map of Greenwood and began to pray over the map every day. Then it occurred to me that I couldn't just pray over a map but that I'd need to start actually visiting Greenwood and learning to know some of the people here. Call me a rocket scientist," Jim quipped.

"So I started driving around the neighborhood, stopping in at churches and shops, meeting people. I brought my daughter, Sara, to a diner here on Saturdays. One day, a group of local folks stopped in during a neighborhood cleanup project, and we asked if we could join in. We spent that beautiful fall day working and laughing with them.

"Another time at the diner, Sara and I started talking to a guy in a suit and tie. He told us he was from Jersey. He'd spent the morning scouting factory locations for his company and had just given up. He told me he realized that this was the wrong neighborhood.

"Here was my first surprise, " Jim declared. "That man's comment really ticked me off. I'd spent enough time hanging around here that his bias against Greenwood felt like a bias against me! If all he saw were problems, then he wasn't looking right!"

The stoical faces had warmed up to the presentation again.

"I told him I thought he could do very well here and that I'd line up some contacts for him if he'd like. So I arranged for him to meet several businessmen interested in his product and got him together with a couple of local community leaders who were eager to provide incentives for him to move here. Long story short, he changed his plans. As we speak, he's in the process of relocating his manufacturing operation right here in Greenwood. A hundred and twenty new jobs will grow out of this."

Applause and a few hoots.

"And what's the hook? We have an incredible asset—an available, trainable workforce and a world-class job-training organization. Dorothy agreed just yesterday to put an Aslan training branch right into his new facility to deliver those workers."

Cheers again, this time acknowledging Dorothy.

"A few other things have happened, too," Jim went on. "I was telling a friend a while back about my prayers for Greenwood—she's a representative of Big Brothers/Big Sisters—and she told me about Dr. Turner's work with children of prisoners. Well, I got right on that since I'd met quite a number of incredible Greenwood community leaders by that time. Short of it is, we've now activated a hundred and fifty mentors from local churches for kids in the Greenwood area.

"Like I said, Bob," Jim continued, smiling broadly, "you're a money grubber! And do you want to know where my family and I have just decided to move?" he asked, his voice combative and playful.

"Greenwood," was Dad's simple answer. "You owe me a hundred bucks, Jim," he added. There were tears in his eyes.

"Glad to pay it," Jim replied, his voice suddenly missing the tone of bravado that had characterized his report. "I feel like I'm living for something now," he added, struggling to control his emotions.

There were several other exciting reports during our meeting. A group of churches in the city is working together to help their members learn about their gifts and passions and then "mobilizing" them strategically in the community. New businesses are forming. Several neighborhood groups are being trained in community organizing skills to increase their effectiveness in addressing neighborhood challenges. A dads' group is teaching young fathers how to be fathers. They're finding some of these absent dads by hanging out in maternity wards where the guys sneak in to try to get a look at their babies! This excited me a lot—even "AWOL" dads often want to see their children.

Dr. Turner updated the group on the mentoring program for children of prisoners. The pastor of the church where we were meeting reported on the church's success in obtaining a nonprofit designation for a new computer skills program for the neighborhood. And several other members of the group shared some new ideas, asking for guidance or direction as they pursued their vision.

The last forty-five minutes was spent in prayer. The most moving part for me was when the group surrounded Dad and prayed for his healing. "Heal him here," the host pastor prayed, his hands on Dad's shoulders. "Or heal him there. But heal him for sure!"

Heal him for sure. That's my prayer, too.

I added to my picture tonight.

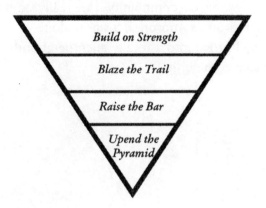

Serving Leadership upends the pyramid, it raises the bar, and it blazes the trail. But it does something else that's very important. It builds on strength. And now I understand what my dad's been saying to me about new eyes. You can't build on strength if you can't see the strength—if all you see is the weakness. To be a Serving Leader, you need new eyes!

Dad's No-Name Team is a strength finder. And a strength connector. Moving from great teams and organizations—established by great Serving Leaders in all areas of business, government, and social sector work—Dad's team aligns strengths for the good of whole communities. This is exciting!

Weeks ago, Martin Goldschmidt had said this to me: "Community happens when everyone rolls up their sleeves and gets to work. Only a Serving Leader can catalyze that kind of a miracle!"

I *saw* what he meant today. More to the point, I felt a part of community today. I feel like I belong and that I have strengths to contribute. I also feel that my weaknesses can be covered by others. It's another paradox, really. You can't become the best unless others do, too. Our best requires their best. We need a community if we really want to shine. "Lone Star" is an oxymoron. If a star is alone, it can't shine.

Today, I drove into a totally alien neighborhood and I experienced community!

ACTION:
RUN TO GREAT PURPOSE

Dad and I lay low yesterday. Our trip to Greenwood pretty much wiped him out, though he's adamant about the fact that it was *not* his last hurrah. To prove it, he set up another appointment for lunch today. "It'll be a very important visit, Son," he told me.

We spent some of our day yesterday in the basement together, working on some final track hookup. Dad mostly watched, though he did touch up a few buildings with paint. We turned the whole system on and ran our trains. For a little while, time stood still—Dad and his boy just played with trains. I'll cherish this memory.

We also talked.

"What's up with Anna?" he asked at one point, a small twinkle in his eyes.

"Nothing," I replied a little defensively. "I don't think anything's up. She's nice, though," I decided to allow.

"Indeed. Like I said to you before. You need new eyes, my boy. *Nothing*, you say!"

I just looked at him, unable to suppress a small smile. Okay, maybe not nothing.

"I've steered clear of relationships for a long time, Pop," I assured him.

"That's supposed to assure me?" he asked, looking very unimpressed. "Trouble is, if you make a habit of steering clear of relationships, you can end up disconnected from everything, including yourself.

"God, too," he added, his eyes piercing me from out over the top of his reading glasses.

I also spent part of yesterday with Mom. Dad napped part of the afternoon, and I helped Mom with a grocery store run and with a couple of other errands. I was glad for the time to talk just with her, to talk about the future, hers without Dad and mine in light of what I've been learning. I'm realizing that this little visit to Philadelphia isn't little at all. My future won't be the same. For one thing, Mom is going to need much more support from me. I need to figure out how this is going to work.

All right, Mike. Time to get back to business.

I helped Dad to the car late this morning, and he surprised me by directing me to Philly's naval shipyard.

"I think you're developing a good model of what a Serving Leader does," Dad said. "But I still think you are missing a key piece. You've got the dynamics of it—how the leader builds the team, the business, and the community—but you're missing something very important. I believe that my friend Admiral Butler can help you with this."

"An admiral is going to teach me something about Serving Leadership?" I asked, a small note of incredulity slipping past my efforts to suppress it.

"Indeed!" he retorted. "I'm going to introduce you today to an admiral in the United States Navy who is a wonderful Serving Leader. You've got to keep your eyes open, Mike," he added. "Great men and women show up everywhere. You'll find them among the poor, and you'll find them among the powerful. But you won't find them if you're not looking for them!"

I felt duly chastised by this remark. Dad's on what turns out to be a pretty full-time mission to heal my blindness, and I admit to the infirmity. I need to keep my eyes open.

Arriving at the shipyard, we were cleared through security, handed passes, and escorted to a squeaky clean boardroom to meet Admiral "Rock" Butler. They had just brought in lunch, and places were set for the three of us.

"Admiral Butler," I said in greeting, a bit cowed by the man's high rank. "It's an honor."

"Call me Rock, please, Mike," he answered. "Everybody else does."

"Okay," I answered doubtfully, not quite ready to address this famous man as my old bud Rock.

Admiral Butler looked to be about fifty-five years old. He was not a big man, standing maybe five foot ten, but his presence was big. The best way I can describe it is that he was at home inside himself. His posture was completely relaxed, but there wasn't a single degree of slouch in his stance. He seemed in full command of his domain but without any particular exertion required. His hair was short and gray, and his face and eyes were as open as those of anyone I've ever met.

"I'd like you to talk to Mike about your approach to leadership, Rock," Dad said, wholly uncowed. "Give him the scoop."

"Before I do that, Mike," Rock replied, "brief me on what you've learned so far about Serving Leaders."

Dad shifted his full attention my way, looking pleased that the admiral had chosen to start out this way.

"Well," I stammered, feeling like I did when Dad put me on the spot back on my very first morning, "Serving Leaders are living paradoxes," I began.

Dad gave me a smile for that line.

"They are leaders who begin by turning the old hierarchy on its head and then placing themselves at the bottom. I'm calling that point *Upend the Pyramid*. They serve many people by first selectively serving a few, and they set high standards for their people. BioWorks calls this *Raise the Bar*. But then they help their people reach those high standards by teaching them how to succeed and by removing obstacles from in front of them. I'm calling this *Blaze the Trail*. And, finally, they help their teams focus on and align along their best strengths. And I'm calling this final point *Build on Strength*.

I stopped. "I guess that's the sixty-second elevator speech," I added, not feeling that I had quite captured it.

"A fair speech," Admiral Butler said equably. "Can you draw it for me?" he asked, pointing to the whiteboard on one side of the boardroom.

I stood, picked up a dark green dry-erase marker and sketched my upside-down pyramid, filling in the four actions I had just mentioned. When I finished the job, I sat down, feeling like a student waiting to get his grade.

Rock stared at the board for a moment, his face inscrutable, and then he turned toward me. "I like it," he began. "I agree with each point you've written there, and I teach them all to my leadership team here."

"Wow!" was all I could think to say. I glanced over at my dad, whose face was as unreadable as Rock's. I turned my attention back to Rock. "So you think I really am getting the important points?" I asked, fishing for one more round of confirmation.

"Well," Rock drawled, a kind smile slowly blooming on his face, "I think you're getting *many* of the important points. But I also think you're missing something that's very important."

"My dad said the same thing this morning, Admiral."

"You really are building a good model," he said encouragingly. "And I think I can help you flesh it out. And, Mike?" he continued. "It's *Rock*, okay?"

"Okay," I said. "You know, Rock," I added, emboldened to try my hand at this "Rock" business, "Dr. Martin Goldschmidt and I talked briefly about what drives the Serving Leader. He said that for him there has to be a larger purpose underneath all the techniques."

"Bingo! That's just what I want to talk with you about." He stood, took a marker, and wrote a phrase in large, bold letters underneath my pyramid.

Run to Great Purpose

Then he underlined the words.

"Let's talk about these words," Rock said, again taking his seat. "I think that Serving Leaders are people in pursuit of a great purpose," he began. "Not something puny but something really important. Important enough to live for. Important enough to die for."

I wrote his words down in my journal.

"What separates Serving Leaders from ordinary leaders is that they're on the trail of such a purpose—it's why I use the word *run*. Serving Leaders articulate a purpose so compelling that people are willing to run toward it. The leaders set the pace, and this spirit gets transferred to the people they serve.

"The thing about your model," he continued, "is that it doesn't have the right foundation." He let that comment stand for a second.

"I have to say it more strongly," Rock added. "Your model doesn't have *any* foundation. It's comprised of several excellent action steps, but what holds it all together?"

I just blinked. "Purpose?" I offered, feeling dumb. He had just told me it was purpose so what was I going to say?

Rock smiled, leaned over, and slapped me on the back. "Tell you what," he said. "I'll do a better job helping you out with this if I can tell you a story. And I need to take you upstairs for that. Are you up for a hike, Bob?" he asked my dad. "Mike and I will help you."

"Count me in," Dad replied, an old soldier's grim determination on his face.

"I want to take you up to what we call 'the Crow's Nest,'" Rock said, reaching into his briefcase to retrieve something. It was an old, weathered Bible. As I processed this, I rose to help Dad.

After navigating a series of stairs and walkways, we ended up inside a glass lookout atop a high wall from which we could see the busy naval port.

Rock started the discussion. "I thought you'd appreciate this. From here you can see the Pyramid Club, where I understand you started this journey." I turned around and looked out across the city, thinking about how far I had come.

Admiral Butler sat down at a small table in the lookout, pulling chairs up for Dad and me. "My role model for this business of great purpose is found in one of the oldest management texts in the world," he stated significantly, laying his old copy of the Bible onto the table between us. "The text is Nehemiah."

"It's in the Old Testament, Mike," Dad said.

"I know it's in the Old Testament," I replied a little testily, hoping Rock wasn't going to ask me to actually find it.

Rock just chuckled, opening his Bible in one flip of the pages right to the place. Dad peeked over at me, eyebrows arched, with a Mona Lisa smile of satisfaction on his face.

"Nehemiah was a senior executive," Rock began, "working in the court of a conquering king, far away from his home city of Jerusalem. He heard about the terrible condition of Jerusalem and felt called to the purpose of rebuilding its walls and gates."

"A slightly bigger task than rebuilding our communities here in Philly," Dad interjected.

"I wouldn't be too sure, Bob. Rebuilding an urban community is the most daunting purpose I know—it's harder than what we do here. Don't sell yourself short," he added.

Dad nodded his acceptance of the correction.

"Anyway, Nehemiah went courageously to the king of Babylon—that's roughly Iraq today—and asked for permission to return to his native city to begin work."

I was taking notes as fast as my hand could move.

"To get a view like we have here from the Crow's Nest, Nehemiah rode around the city, all the way around it, late at night, seeing for himself the damage and devastation. Compelled by the purpose in his heart, he presented a dramatic vision to his people of restoration of the twelve gates and interlocking walls of Jerusalem to their former splendor. At the same time, he was a realist, seeing the extensive damage before him. It would be an effort requiring the co-operation of everyone in Jerusalem.

"You see that, Mike?" Rock asked. "He had a great purpose. And he knew that *the solution would require everyone's best strength*. That's one of your key points."

I underlined it in my journal.

"The next day," Rock continued, "he brought together the elders and leaders of the city and gave them a purpose and a challenge, to restore Jerusalem to its former glory.

"Then came, what did you call it, the upside-down pyramid?"

"Upending the Pyramid," I answered.

"Right. Nehemiah divided the work according to families—families who were living adjacent to the damaged gates and walls—and then he *upended the pyramid* and put all his time into helping them succeed at their great task."

I underlined that, too.

"Soon critics and enemies of the rebuilding came out of the woodwork, threatening the workers. Nehemiah's role shifted again as a Serving Leader to providing physical and spiritual protection."

I scribbled *Blaze the Trail* in the margin here.

"The work proceeded to full success," Rock concluded, "because they were running with Nehemiah toward his great purpose; it had totally captured their hearts. One by one, the gates and walls were restored."

"I get it," I declared, nodding.

"It's my job right now," Rock replied, "to make sure that you do get it. And so I want to make my point even sharper. You've got a great model. It matches my own learning and experience profoundly well. But *purpose* isn't the final point, Mike." He stated this emphatically, and I just stared at him. Was there *another* point?

"Purpose is your *first* point!" Rock concluded. "Upend the Pyramid? Why? Raise the Bar to what end? Blaze the

Trail so people can get where? Build on Strength to achieve what?"

He let the questions hang in the air, and we looked at each other.

"If the purpose isn't bigger than the people involved, none of the great things you're seeing here in Philadelphia would be happening. People need an answer to the purpose question, and, contrary to what most people believe, self-interest isn't the answer that really delivers, and it isn't the answer that really satisfies."

Rock paused again and looked at me. I looked back. I was thinking. People need an answer to the purpose question, Rock had just said. So what has been *my* answer?

To get promoted; that's been one of my answers for a very long time. To get a bigger salary. Maybe win the boss's job. To get to the top. These have been my answers. And how empty they all seem right now. I could have stayed on that path, achieved every goal, totally succeeded, and ended up exactly where I started—still wondering why.

"None of the incredible acceleration and creative teamwork and high productivity your model speaks of will happen," Rock continued, "unless you build your model on top of the foundation of a great purpose. Get that clear first, and everything else will follow!

"Are you there, Mike?" he then asked, apparently unsure what was going on behind my glazed eyes.

"Oh, I'm here," I answered, chuckling and shaking my head. "It's just that I'm a little occupied right now rearranging all the furniture in my brain."

Rock smiled and nodded. He was more than satisfied.

I looked over at Dad, and there were tears running down his cheeks. The look on his face told me that what had just happened pleased him beyond words.

Run to Great Purpose is the *first* action that marks the Serving Leader. It's the foundation. Everything else follows.

"Okay, Rock," I said, clearing my throat. "I'll change my model. I haven't any doubt about it; Run to Great Purpose is the *first* action that marks the Serving Leader. It's the foundation. Everything else follows." I made this comment with absolute clarity of mind and real conviction.

"Mike, it's going to be a pleasure learning to know you better," Rock said. His face told me that he meant every word of it. "And, Bob," he added, turning to my dad, "a chip off the old block is how I see it."

Dad's tears continued to flow, his face a portrait of gratitude.

"I'm thinking about your No-Name Team, Dad," I said, turning to face him squarely. He wiped his eyes. "They're connected at such a deep level. It's more than the techniques they're using. They have a purpose that pulls everything into focus. It helps me understand why such great people want to be on the team, where the morale comes from, and why I see such courage in the circle."

Dad nodded.

"They want to make a real difference for Philadelphia. For everybody who lives here. They believe they *can*."

"That's the whole point, Mike," Rock said. "Making a difference for others is the point of our lives. It is the great purpose that gives us everything we need to run the best race we can." His voice trailed off. He kept his eyes focused on me, his face deeply thoughtful.

"Has anyone told you before that you were born to make a difference?"

I held Rock's gaze, considering his question. No one

had ever told me that, exactly. I really wanted to believe it and felt ready to.

"You were born to make a difference, Mike," Rock repeated. It wasn't a question this time. "And I see no reason why you shouldn't start today. Start right now," he added, his voice quiet and commanding.

No one said anything for a long moment, and then I nodded my head.

"This is an important day for me, Admiral," I said. "And you were right, Dad. I was missing an important piece. My model was missing it, and so was I.

"Can I ask you both a question?" I continued. "While we're dealing with missing pieces?"

"Ask," Dad responded.

"How does the spiritual part work? Or more precisely, is the spiritual part required for Serving Leadership to work? You both carry around Bibles."

"It's important to me, Mike," Dad said, his voice quavering with emotion. "My faith is important to me because it keeps me in mind of the fact that my life doesn't belong to me. My living needs to serve something bigger than myself."

"I know that's true of you, Dad," I answered, wondering why he was explaining this to me. I knew it full well.

"I want it to be true of you, too, Mike," Dad continued, his face now full of feeling.

"It *is* true of me," I answered strongly, now understanding how he had taken my question. He thought I was back to my personal ruminations, which at this moment I wasn't. "It's *becoming* true of me, I should say. If you're troubled about my part in this, you can put your mind at ease. I'm on the way." I walked over to where my dad was sitting and gave him a hug. I really appreciated how much he cared for me, for the whole of me.

"You were really asking *two* questions, weren't you, Mike?" Rock said. "One of a personal nature and one more professional."

"Thank you, Rock, for saying that so well," I answered, glad for the graceful transition he offered. "I work with a lot of clients, and I need to provide business value regardless of a client's spiritual orientation or nonorientation. I want to promote principles and actions that can be applied in many different settings and that work for many different kinds of people. Some of them are spiritually inclined, to be sure. And some have deeply humane principles that aren't religiously motivated. And some are driven to build great and profitable companies. So, yes, my question is, does Serving Leadership just plain work?"

"It just plain works," Dad answered. Rock nodded. "Many of our friends are from different faiths," Dad continued, "and many of the firms that use our principles have no faith agenda."

"We have colleagues in government," Rock added, "who are reporting great benefit from Serving Leadership. I use these principles right here in my Navy post."

"I guess I loaded up your schedule with a lot of the more faith-oriented colleagues, Mike," my dad then said, a grin of confession on his face. "A father's prerogative."

"But here's the point," Rock continued. "Bring great purpose to the table, turn your leadership into service to your workers, hold high expectations, make sure your team has what it needs in training and resources and clear running ground, and maximize the strengths you have. Take these actions, and you'll get real acceleration and impact. We believe it's how we've been designed to function best."

"Faith or no faith," Dad added.

"Whether working with a small team, working with an entire corporation, or working with all the sectors of a great city," Rock said.

"Live it out very personally, or set the principles in motion at a large corporate level. Let it bring deep private meaning to your life and to your family, or let it produce great public value," Dad added. "Better yet, do both."

Both men paused.

"But please don't steer clear of God in your own life, Mike," Dad continued. "Your father speaking here. Serving Leadership requires a deep humility and a willingness to pour yourself into the good of others. I pray that you let yourself be nurtured for this by something larger than yourself."

"Your dad is offering you excellent counsel," Rock said, his face sober. "Leaders find themselves in very difficult places. Great leaders do," he added.

"Admiral, Dad," I said, "you've answered my questions and then some. I want to make a difference with my life. And I want to help many, many others excel in their leadership so their lives can also make a difference. Thank you."

"I've enjoyed it, Mike," the Admiral said, rising to his feet. "But can I give you one more piece of advice?"

"Sure," I said, rising to join him.

"Call me Rock," he said, this time with a very wide smile.

"Rock," I replied, nodding firmly.

The Admiral gave me a big hug.

I picked up my notebook, which was an almost unreadable scribble of notes, filled with whole sections of Rock's remarks that I tried to capture word for word, as well as sidebar notations. I knew I was going to have my hands full getting it down more clearly later.

Not to mention the job of actually living it out. That's going to make the job of writing it all down a cinch in comparison.

I looked over at my dad, who had not yet gotten out of his seat. He looked back at me with eyes that were suddenly very tired. And very content.

Rock wanted a few final minutes just with my father, and I took the opportunity to reflect on what I had just heard, what it meant for my own life, and something that was still troubling me.

In the car, I asked Dad one remaining question. Given my own track record, was I fit to be a Serving Leader? He knew exactly what I needed to hear.

"We've all made mistakes and wasted lots of time and talent, Mike," he said, reaching over to lay his hand on my arm.

"But mistakes aren't the issue. What you do with them is the issue."

I nodded.

"We're all faced with three choices," he continued. "First, we can pretend that everything's always been just fine. If we make this choice, we have to spend all our time putting on a front for people, acting like we have it all together, and making up excuses for our meaningless lives."

Dad let the point hang in the air. I was thinking about the times I'd behaved just this way.

"We become smaller people when we do this, Mike. We're justified in our own minds but useless to anyone else.

"Secondly, and just as bad, we can destroy ourselves in lament and self-recrimination. We've wasted too much of our lives, it's too late to get on track now, and so we don't really deserve another chance to become really strong and great."

This description, actually, fit my condition better than the first one, I realized. Dad had just cut to the quick of my fundamental struggle.

"Again, this is wrong, and just makes us small. What good can a groveling, self-whipped soul be to anyone else?" he asked, the question needing no answer.

"And the third one, Dad?" I asked, trying to hide how desperately I needed to hear a better option.

Dad squeezed my arm. "Ask to be forgiven for the past, Mike. And then seize your future with all you've got. Join the team!"

It wasn't clear to me if he was just giving me his third point or if he was giving me a command.

I liked it either way. I was ready.

THE SERVING LEADER

Ali suggested I try my hand at writing a job description for the Serving Leader. Though it's been nearly two months since I finished this journal, rereading it now confirms in my mind that it captures reasonably well the key elements of what I learned from my father and his friends—well, *my* friends now, too. There is much to flesh out, of course, but I've not really had time lately to do it. I think I'm ready to give it a try.

Hey, Dad! Take a look!

SERVING LEADERS

- *Run to great purpose* by holding out in front of their team, business, or community a "reason why" that is so big that it requires and motivates everybody's very best effort.

- *Upend the pyramid* of conventional management thinking. They put themselves at the bottom of the pyramid and unleash the energy, excitement, and talents of the team, the business, and the community.

- *Raise the bar* of expectation by being highly selective in the choice of team leaders and by establishing high standards of performance. These actions build a culture of performance throughout the team, business, or community.

- *Blaze the trail* by teaching Serving Leader principles and practices and by removing obstacles to performance. These actions multiply the Serving Leader's impact by educating and activating tier after tier of leadership.

- *Build on strength* by arranging each person in the team, the business, and the community to contribute what he or she is best at. This improves everyone's performance and solidifies teams by aligning the strengths of many people.

The whole time I was working on this—from my first day at the Pyramid Club to my last day with Rock in the Crow's Nest—I was scratching down notes about the paradoxes of Serving Leadership. Dad had urged me to watch for them, and the more I watched, the more I saw. What do you have to say about these paradoxes, Dad? Not too bad a list, huh?

THE SERVING LEADER—A PARADOX IN AND OF ITSELF!

Run to Great Purpose
To do the most possible good, strive for the impossible. Sustain the self's greatest interest in pursuits beyond self-interest.

Upend the Pyramid
You qualify to be first by putting other people first.
You're in charge principally to charge up others.

Raise the Bar
To serve the many, you first serve the few.
The best reach-down is a challenging reach-up.

Blaze the Trail
To protect your value, you must give it all away.
Your biggest obstacle is the one that hinders someone else.

Build on Strength
To address your weaknesses, focus on your strengths.
You can't become the best unless others do, too.

I don't feel there's a lot more to write down. Except to say that I wish my dad *could* read these lines.

Dad died a month ago. Since then, I've been pretty busy rearranging my life. I've also spent quite a bit of time just hanging out—with Charlie and my crew in Boston some, with my friends in Philadelphia more, with Mom a lot, and mostly with myself. I have so much to reflect on right now, and I don't want to jet right through this period of my life. I'm taking the train.

I miss my dad.

I write that sentence, and it looks like a sentence I've been writing in one way or another my whole lifetime. Except it's very different now. I used to miss Dad, wondering what he thought of me, wondering if he was proud of me, wondering how much he loved me. I had literally *missed* him. Our lives didn't hit, we hadn't connected.

Now I miss being with the man whose life I had the good fortune of not missing. I miss the man who knew and loved me greatly. Indeed, I don't feel I've missed anything, if that makes sense. Dad and I finished what was important to finish, and now I have a lifetime ahead to try to honor his life, and my own. I miss him, but he feels very, very close.

Dad failed very quickly after our day with Rock. It was his time, and I honestly think he felt like he had finished the race—his lifelong, flat-out, chest-first sprint to the tape. I spent every waking hour with him those last three and a half weeks, and more than a few sleeping hours at the hospital, too. Mom and I celebrated his seventieth birthday at his bedside. A quiet celebration. Dad was in and out of consciousness that day, but Mom and I weren't going to miss the moment. If Dad was going to finish strong, then so were we!

Robert Taylor Wilson. July 27, 1933 to August 3, 2003. Survived by his wife of forty-seven years, Margaret Shoemaker Wilson of Philadelphia, Pennsylvania, and by one son, Robert Michael Wilson of Boston, Massachusetts. It's remarkable how little gets recorded in the end.

As per Dad's instructions, his headstone added the spare notation: "A Serving Leader, Matthew 20:25–28." I looked it up.

But Jesus called them to him and said, "You know that the rulers of the Gentiles lord it over them, and their great men exercise authority over them. It shall not be so among you; but whoever would be great among you must be your servant, and whoever would be first among you must be your slave; even as the Son of man came not to be served but to serve, and to give his life as a ransom for many."

One correction is needed; it isn't Robert Michael Wilson of Boston, Massachusetts, anymore. It's Robert Michael

Wilson of Philadelphia, Pennsylvania—of Greenwood, to be more specific. Dorothy Hyde and I negotiated a modest office suite inside Aslan's new branch in Greenwood for me and a couple of coworkers from my firm. I'm practicing my new skills of careful selection, à la the Serving Leader model. With Charlie's blessing, we're locating our new leadership development practice in this office, and I was allowed to interview throughout the firm to select team leaders who grasp how promising this Serving Leader model is.

We're committed to introduce our clients to the principles practiced by the Dorothy Hydes and Admiral Butlers of the world. My new crew has joined me in this purpose. We have continued to work on our upside-down model of leadership—our Serving Leader Pyramid. Here's the picture we use, reorganized with "Purpose" at the foundation.

THE SERVING LEADER

Build on Strength

Blaze the Trail

Raise the Bar

Upend the Pyramid

Run to Great Purpose

In response to Rock's challenge, I have chosen to serve those leaders who are committed to becoming Serving Leaders in their businesses and communities. It all crystallized for me—Dad's example, Rock's challenge, all the inspiration I received from Dorothy Hyde. It has become the passion of my heart.

Greenwood serves us in remarkable ways. It keeps the crew and me immersed in the best living laboratory we could find. The very principles we will teach and coach are found in the heart of this community. Dad called Greenwood our best hope, and I understand now what he meant.

Innovation takes place rapidly in places like Greenwood. With the freedom afforded by "nothing left to lose," Serving Leaders like Dorothy Hyde are fearless in improving their practices. Failure is allowed. Experimentation, innovation, and perseverance are their lifeblood. These qualities are their stock-in-trade. What better place is there to stay ahead of the curve?

There are other reasons to be here, too. Mom needs me. I'm going to stake my reputation as a Serving Leader on whether I am one as her son. It seems only fair.

And, okay, there's Anna. Yes, she keeps calling and stopping by. And, yes, I've also been calling and stopping by. And, well, we'll see. That's really all I want to say about that. If Dad were reading this, I'm sure he'd be issuing his customary snort right about now.

Well, then, finally, this was my place of birth, and in a real sense, the place of my birth again. In Boston, I had an apartment, an office, and air connections to many disconnected places. And that was important and good. I'm not changing everything. I sense that I'm not supposed to waste all that training and preparation. I'm a consultant—and I'm pretty good at it. I want to build on that rather than to throw it away.

But in Philadelphia, I'm rooted in community. I'm rooted in important relationships, and I want it this way!

Hey, Dad, I'm thinking right now that you probably are reading this, just to see how it finishes up. I hope that you are. Charlie said I should write this journal so we could turn it into something useful for our clients. Maybe we'll still do that, but, frankly, Dad, I can't imagine any greater satisfaction than I felt the day I watched your face as you read through some of these pages. I saw it in your eyes—your love for me and the value you placed on my life.

So, Dad, thank you. You ran a great race. I will finish what you started!

ACKNOWLEDGMENTS

It is not possible to give all the credit we owe to Serving Leaders, authors, researchers, friends, and family who have informed, inspired, and loved us.

The civil and human rights organization Focus: HOPE was the inspiration for Aslan Industries in our story. Led by cofounder Eleanor Josaitis, Focus: HOPE began in 1968 as a response to Detroit's devastating violence. Offering nationally recognized technical training and education, Focus: HOPE works with corporations and universities to provide world-class education to the city's economically poorest young people. Focus: HOPE is also deeply involved in community development initiatives, promoting the arts and operating a childcare center on its campus in the heart of Detroit. Visit the group at www.focushope.edu.

The Amachi Initiative inspired the "children of prisoners" mentoring program in our story. Founded and led by former Philadelphia mayor the Reverend Dr. Wilson Goode Sr., Amachi has united churches, Big Brothers/Big Sisters, Public/Private Ventures, the Center for Research on Religion and Urban Civil Society, and the Robert A. Fox Leadership Program at the University of Pennsylvania. Amachi breaks the cycle of hopelessness faced by many children of prisoners who can imagine no other future but that of their own eventual incarceration. Learn more about Amachi at www.ppv.org.

Leadership Foundations of America (LFA) inspired the No-Name Team. Founded and led by Reid Carpenter, LFA works in dozens of cities to bring leaders together from every sector to address our society's most besetting problems of poverty, injustice, and human degradation. To give one example, Fresno, California's No-Name Fellowship and the One by One Leadership Foundation demonstrate the principles of this book in an exemplary way. Visit Leadership Foundations of America at www.LFofA.org.

Special thanks to Ken and Margie Blanchard for their friendship and their pioneering vision "to unleash the potential and power of people and organizations for the common good." The Blanchards lead one of the most influential full-service management consulting and training organizations in the world (www.kenblanchardcompanies.com). With his lifelong friend Phil Hodges, Ken has established an exemplary Serving Leadership initiative whose goal is to teach people to "Lead Like Jesus" (www. faithwalkleadership.org).

Bob Buford, author of *Halftime*, has stimulated a national movement of many successful men and women who, like Mike Wilson, feel that their lives lack significance. A friend and an inspiration, Bob's work and his commitment to service make a huge difference in our world. Visit Bob at www.halftime.org.

Long before Bruce Wilkinson wrote his profound book, *The Prayer of Jabez*, an Episcopal priest named Samuel Moor Shoemaker moved to Pittsburgh and inspired a similar marketplace prayer movement called "The Pittsburgh Experiment." Building on his prior pioneering work in New York City with Alcoholics Anonymous and Faith at Work (www.faithatwork.com), Shoemaker gathered business sector leaders in the 1950s and taught them how to pray and then act on behalf of their city. Visit them at www.pghexp.org. Without this fifty-year effort in Pittsburgh, this book would not exist.

Though all the characters in our story are purely fictitious, some may bear a resemblance to friends who inspire us. These include Newt Crenshaw, Bill Dempsey, Craig Esterly, Ali Hanna, W. Wilson Goode, Eleanor Josaitis, Ali Walker, and Doug Wilson—Serving Leaders all. Any positive characteristics found in this book may be attributed to each of these persons. Character flaws that may be found in this story reflect the character flaws of the authors alone.

We are grateful to Jim Collins for his rigorous research and recent book, *Good to Great: Why Some Companies Make the Leap and Others Don't*. Collins's research includes the effectiveness of Serving Leadership. Noel Tichy and Andy McGill demonstrate the power of a "teachable point of view" through the Global Leadership Program at the University of Michigan.

Our friend and counsel Dr. Alistair Hanna generously encouraged us and gave us a view into his inspiring life. A trusted advisor to many Fortune 500 companies, he built a legendary career that led him to the top of McKinsey and Company. Not stopping there, he went on to found Alpha North America, a ministry to help people find the meaning of life. Alpha offers a course of investigation into the validity and relevance of Christianity and a practical introduction to a relationship with Jesus Christ for people from all backgrounds. Alpha courses are offered throughout the continent and have reached over a million people. You can learn more about Alpha at www.alphausa.org.

Mentors, friends, and clients who have taught us along the way include Ray Bakke, Bryan Barry, Harold Bauman, Titus Bender, Bruce Bickel, Justin Brown, Greg Bunch, Charles Butler, Kevin Butler, Reid Carpenter, Terry Collier, Mary Crimmins, Andrea Cruz, Lisa Cummins, George Francis, Nelson Good, Ginger Graham, Terri Lyn Greene, Rosie Grier, Brad Henderson, John Hirt, Dick Johnson, Scott Keffer, Jessica King, James Lapp, Larry Lenihan, Doug Lind, Alec Litowitz, Russ Lloyd, Deb Magness, Glenn Main III, Sharyn Materna, Colvin McCrady, Tom McGeHee, Judy Messina, Kurt Miller, David Mosey, Jim Mudd, Marilyn Mulvihill, Paul Olson, Bill Pasmore, Karen Plavan, Jace Ransom, Don and B. J. Russell, Paul Schaut, Arden Shank, Amy Sherman, Kirk Shisler, Marisa Smucker, H. Spees, Bill Starr, Dale Stoltzfus, Lynn Summers, Lisa Thorpe-Vaughn, Don Uber, Rick Wellock, Terry White, and Tom Wilson, to name only a few.

Thanks to Dr. George Brushaber (Bethel College) and Dr. James Dittmar (Geneva College) for the vision and courage to make Serving Leadership relevant to executive education and leadership training.

Valerie Andrews, Beverly Butterfield, Sharon Goldinger, Tom Heuerman, Chris Lee, Catherine Nomura, Perry Pascarella—and most especially Steve Piersanti—read and reread this manuscript with incredible dedication to its improvement. The entire team at Berrett-Koehler, led by Piersanti, exemplifies the principles reflected in this book. We hope you see the fruit of your labor!

Love and eternal thanks to Milonica, life partner and encourager for John in this writing endeavor, as in all others. And to daughters Emma and Clara for daily supplying a big and happy answer to the question "Why?"

Ken's family provided many insights, inspirations, and challenges along his path to understanding the heart of a Serving Leader.

Blessings and love to J. J., David, Matt, and Sara. Heather protects and serves so Ken can travel, work, and live a life worth living.

While this book was being conceived, Ken's dad, a World War II veteran in his 70s, led a team of church members to restore homes near New York's "Ground Zero." Service like this is an example of how leadership arises to meet every need and knows no territory. Love to Mom and Dad.

STRATEGIC RESOURCES

VentureWorks

Founded by a coauthor of this book, Ken Jennings, VentureWorks provides consulting and coaching for both companies and nonprofit organizations. The VentureWorks Process provides effective approaches to Strategy Execution, Executive Coaching, as well as Leadership and Team Development. The VentureWorks Process is unique in its integration of Serving Leadership principles and leading-edge approaches to organizational effectiveness.
Ken.Jennings@VentureWorks.org; www. ventureworks.org

Center for FaithWalk Leadership

The Center for FaithWalk Leadership was founded by Ken Blanchard and Phil Hodges to challenge and equip people to "Lead Like Jesus." Work with those you influence in a way that honors God and the individual. Learn how a new perspective on an old, proven concept of leadership will transform you and give you the results you have always wanted in your ministry or corporation. www.faithwalkleadership.org

Half Time

Halftime.org is an interactive tool that is made available by Bob Buford, author of *Halftime*. It was designed to serve participants on their halftime journey by providing helpful hints, personal stories, outstanding resources (newsletters, personal coaching, recommended books, articles, and events), and specific next steps for those who are interested in embracing significance. www.halftime.org

The Strategic Coach Inc.

The Strategic Coach offers entrepreneurs practical tools and strategies that allow them to focus their unique talents and passions and those of their team members to create breakthrough results, personally and professionally. Entrepreneurs and their teams learn to set and achieve big goals, package and share their wisdom, and overcome obstacles. The Strategic Coach is a secular organization with products and programs appropriate for all entrepreneurial thinkers. www.strategiccoach. com

Pittsburgh Leadership Foundation

Founded as a faith-based organization in 1978, Pittsburgh Leadership Foundation (PLF) works with business, government, and nonprofit leaders to address the needs of youth, persons suffering from addictions, prisoners, and the poor. PLF is also the parent organization of the Council of Leadership Foundations, a fifty-city collaborative of faith-based civic intermediaries who exchange best practices from across the country to increase the capacity of frontline community-based organizations. www.plf.org

COACHING

CoachWorks® International Corporation

CoachWorks is a community of executive leader coaches committed to working with leaders to enhance competencies for changing times, leadership teams to achieve true synergy, and organizations to create better ways of meeting marketplace demands. The coaches are dedicated to long-term success of individuals and organizations through leadership development and executive coaching around Legacy Leadership, the comprehensive CoachWorks leadership model. www.legacyleadership.com; www.coachworks.com

Performaworks

Performaworks provides goal-driven, performance management software that can dramatically improve your organization's ability to execute on its strategy. www.performaworks.com

TheGiftednessCenter℠

Sorting through second-half options is largely a matter of determining, What fits me? Bill Hendricks and TheGiftednessCenter℠ have a long history of helping leaders identify their "sweet spot" and where they should focus their energies. They also answer the team question,

Who else is required to make me effective? Bill and his team excel at getting the people part right. www.thegiftednesscenter.com

Marketplace Ministries

Since 1984, Marketplace Ministries, headquartered in Dallas, Texas, has provided America's premier Employee Care Program (ECP) to 257 client companies from California to Massachusetts. This corporate chaplains' service is caring for more than 250,000 workers and their families. Some 1,250 business chaplains weekly visit 900 work sites in 359 cities spread across thirty-five states. Their work is caring and their care is working. www.marketplaceministries.com

OnCourse International

OnCourse International mentors executives and professionals who face challenging midlife issues. Jim Warner, founder and facilitator, has "walked in the shoes" of leaders so he can empathize with their issues, encouraging them to face change and then helping them chart course corrections for their personal life plan. www.oncoursein.com

Pathfinders

Are you ready to grab the wheel and steer your life beyond survival? Should you go for an "off-the-shelf" job or create something unique? Today, it's possible to have a practical career that also makes a difference. Since 1991, Pathfinders has expertly guided thousands of people in making wise career choices, offering world-class natural ability testing and career coaching programs. www.pathfinders.org

The WildWorks Group

The WildWorks Group dramatically accelerates business results/decisions and people's commitment to change through a unique collaborative experience. By applying a proven methodology, the group designs and conducts a two- to three-day session in a uniquely designed environment that enables the power of all of the participants (thirty to one hundred) to accomplish more together than they could independently. This experience can be applied to various needs, including strategy development, new product launches, and operationalization of strategic initiatives. The group provides this service for businesses, communities, and organizations. www.wildworksgroup.com

FINANCIAL AND LIFE PLANNING RESOURCES

The Main Point LP

The mission of the Main Point is to enable individuals who have significant potential to feel confident about their true wealth, freeing them to contribute to the world at the highest level of their creativity. The company believes it is not what you have or what you do but who you are that leads to your personal main point in life. www.TheMainPointLP.com

Wealth Transfer Solutions, Inc.

You are a philanthropist whether you know it or not. Taxes are a form of philanthropy—involuntary philanthropy. Wealth Transfer Solutions helps affluent individuals, families, and business owners disinherit the Internal Revenue Service in favor of their families and charity. Receive clarity, focus, simplicity—and results—through comprehensive wealth planning and management. skeffer@preserve-wealth.com

Ronald Blue & Co.

Ronald Blue & Co. is a fee-only business providing personalized financial, estate, and investment counsel. It assists clients with managing their financial resources proactively and responsibly so they can experience peace of mind. It can help you address a wide array of halftime issues. www.ronblue.com

Oxford Financial Group

Oxford Financial Group delivers independent investment advice to institutions, not-for-profit organizations, retirement plans, families, and individuals. www.oxfordgroupltd.com

TRAINING CENTERS AND INSTITUTES

The Greenleaf Center for Servant Leadership

The Greenleaf Center's mission is to fundamentally improve the caring and quality of all institutions through a new approach to leadership, structure, and decision making. Servant Leadership emphasizes increased service to others, a holistic approach to work, promotion of a sense of community, and sharing of power in decision making.

Founded in 1964 by Robert K. Greenleaf, author of the seminal book *Servant Leadership*, The Greenleaf Center has pioneered the field and study of Servant Leadership. www.greenleaf.org

Bethel University

The new Bethel School of Leadership, focusing on Applied Servant Leadership, is now being developed. Bethel is committed to creating a new and exciting approach to executive leadership development that combines the best of leadership coaching, strategy execution assistance, and Servant Leadership in action.www.bethel.edu

Geneva College MSOL

The masters of science degree in organizational leadership (MSOL) at Geneva College is designed for working adults and is offered at locations within the greater Pittsburgh area. The ethics of leadership taught within a servant leadership context is a major theme that runs through the curriculum. www.geneva.edu

COMMUNITY DEVELOPMENT AND SERVICE

Christian Community Development Association

The Christian Community Development Association (CCDA) educates, trains, inspires, and nurtures the people who are rebuilding the broken communities of urban America. The distinctiveness of CCDA is its advocating for restoring communities in a biblical-based philosophy, integrating faith into community development activities. CCDA was founded in 1989 by Dr. John Perkins and now serves more than three thousand Christian development practitioners and more than five hundred churches and organizations. www.ccda.org

Impact Urban America

Impact Urban America (IUA) promotes collaboration between the business community, social service organizations, and faith-based organizations to transform America's inner cities. World-renowned author and training and development consultant Ken Blanchard and Impact Urban America recently developed a specially designed life and job skills leadership and accountability program called Impact Training and Development Solutions. www.impacturbanamerica.com

The Gamaliel Foundation

The Gamaliel Foundation is a powerful network of grassroots, interfaith, interracial, multi-issue organizations working together to create a more just and more democratic society. The organizations of the Gamaliel Network allow ordinary people to effectively participate in the political, environmental, social, and economic decisions affecting their lives. The network helps create and sustain such organizations and is the vehicle for these organizations to act on at a national and international level. www.gamaliel.org

Leadership Network

The mission of Leadership Network is to accelerate the emergence of effective churches in the United States and Canada. Acknowledged as an influential leader among churches and faith-based ministries, Leadership Network identifies, connects, and offers resources to strategic leaders and congregations and is a major resource to which innovative leaders turn for networking and information. www.leadnet.org

CONFERENCES/SEMINARS

Serving Leader Workshops. Putting into practice the "5 powerful actions that will transform your team, your business, and your community." www.theservingleader.com

Leadership Foundations of America Training Institute. An annual best-practices institute bringing community and multisector leaders together to address common challenges facing cities everywhere. Topics include community building, fund-raising, economic development, prisoner aftercare, urban youth building, and establishment of multisector collaborations. www.plf.org

Developing Your Game Plan Workshop. Provided by HalfTime, the one-day workshop is designed to focus the participant on critical questions leading to developing a winning game plan for the second half of life. It explores gifts, talents, personal calling, and specific next steps. www.halftime.org

Time Out Model. An annual event in Silicon Valley that brings leaders together to discover God's unique call on their lives and explore how to heed the call. It aims to provide a safe environment for people to (1) reflect on their lives with their peers; (2) work toward balance among all their competing priorities; and (3) invest their resources, talent, and gifts as God leads them for maximum impact in the world. It's a good replicable model for other cities. For more information, contact duane.moyer@faithworks.net

Second Half Ministries. An opportunity to experience, with your spouse, a meaningful midlife review. During three weekend forums, participants are guided through an enriching personal evaluation that becomes the foundation for a development plan for the second half of their lives. Contact the group at (719) 594-2301 or www.gospelcom.net/navs/secondhalf

BOOKS

Bennis, Warren. *On Becoming a Leader.* Cambridge, Mass.: Perseus Publishing, 1994. Management expert Warren Bennis shows how individuals develop leadership traits and how organizations encourage or stifle potential leaders. Bennis profiles dynamic figures from diverse business arenas.

Blanchard, Ken, and Jesse Stoner. *Full Steam Ahead! Unleash the Power of Vision in Your Company and Your Life.* San Francisco: Berrett-Koehler, 2003. Jesse Stoner teams up with Ken Blanchard to take the mystery out of creating a clear, compelling vision for your organization and for yourself. They show where vision comes from, how it unleashes great power and energy, and how it provides ongoing focus and direction.

Blanchard, Ken, Bill Hybels, and Phil Hodges. *Leadership by the Book.* New York: William Morrow, 1999. The authors use a parable to show how the Bible can be applied to leadership in modern organizations.

Blanchard, Ken, John P. Carlos, and Alan Randolph. *The 3 Keys to Empowerment: Release the Power Within People for Astonishing Results.* San Francisco: Berrett-Koehler, 2001. The three keys to empowerment are share information with everyone, create autonomy through boundaries, and let teams become the hierarchy. The book provides an easy-to-follow list of actions leaders can take at each stage of the journey to empowerment.

Block, Peter. *Stewardship: Choosing Service Over Self-Interest.* San Francisco: Berrett-Koehler, 1996. Peter Block takes the principles of Edward Demming and puts them into a usable methodology that will help business owners focus on the essentials for achieving success and inspiring members of the team at all levels.

Bridges, William. *Transitions: Making Sense of Life's Changes.* Cambridge, Mass.: Perseus, 1980. William Bridges explains how to take care of yourself so you can make it through life's bumps and scrapes.

Buckingham, Marcus, and Donald Clifton. *Now Discover Your Strengths.* New York: Free Press, 2001. This book describes the revolutionary new approach to identifing your talents, building them into strengths, and performing at a consistently high level.

Buford, Bob. *Game Plan.* Grand Rapids, Mich.: Zondervan, 1999. The author offers a critical challenge and practical strategies for creating significance in the second half of life.

———. *Halftime: Changing Your Game Plan from Success to Significant.* Grand Rapids, Mich.: Zondervan, 1997. Whether you are a millionaire, a manager, or a teacher, you will one day have to transition from the struggle for success to the quest for significance. "Halftime" is a quiet time of deliberate decision making and restructuring of your heart's deepest desires.

Collins, Jim. *Good to Great: Why Some Companies Make the Leap . . . and Others Don't.* New York: HarperCollins, 2001. Peppered with dozens of stories and examples from the great companies and the not so great, the book offers a well-reasoned road map to excellence.

———. *Level 5 Leadership: The Triumph of Humility and Fierce Resolve.* Cambridge, Mass.: Harvard Business School Press, 2001. Jim Collins paints a compelling and counterintuitive portrait of the skills and personality traits necessary for effective leadership. He identifies the characteristics common to Level 5 leaders: humility, will, ferocious resolve, and the tendency to give credit to others while assigning blame to themselves. Collins fleshes out his Level 5 theory by telling colorful tales about eleven such leaders from recent business history.

DePree, Max. *Leadership Is an Art.* New York: Dell, 1990. Going beyond the mechanics of leading and into the ethics and philosophy of leadership, the book puts a human face on corporate leadership.

Drucker, Peter F. *Managing the Non-profit Organization: Principles and Practices.* San Francisco: Harper Business, 1992. The material is presented simply and concisely and is completely targeted to the nonprofit sector with many examples, including interviews with about six to seven nonprofit leaders.

Gallup, George, Jr., and Timothy Jones. *The Next American Spirituality: Finding God in the Twenty-First Century.* Colorado Springs, Colo.: Chariot Victor Publishers, 2000. Gallup uses poll data to analyze the condition of spirituality in America, focusing on religious activities, including prayer, charitable work, and Bible study.

Gordon, Wayne L. *Real Hope in Chicago.* Grand Rapids, Mich.: Zondervan, 1995. The narratives in this book will tug at your heart and inspire action. Gordon has created a special community by developing leadership from within, supporting basic needs within his neighborhood, and valuing each individual.

Greenleaf, Robert K. *The Power of Servant Leadership.* San Francisco: Berrett-Koehler, 1998. Nearly thirty years ago, Robert Greenleaf wrote clearly and forcefully about servant leadership, pioneering the term. This volume is a great help for stepping into the future that Greenleaf describes so eloquently.

———. *Servant Leadership: A Journey into the Nature of Legitimate Power and Greatness.* New York: Paulist Press, 1977. Robert Greenleaf's compelling insight into the essence of true leadership based on the servant perspective shows how true leaders lead from the front—and the back.

Hesselbein, Frances. *Hesselbein on Leadership.* San Francisco: Jossey-Bass, 2002. In a disarmingly simple manner, Frances Hesselbein spells out nuances and specifics that those atop any private, public, or nonprofit organization would do well to absorb.

Jaworski, Joseph. *Synchronicity: The Inner Path of Leadership.* San Francisco: Berrett-Koehler, 1998. Joseph Jaworski (son of Leon Jaworski, the famous special prosecutor of the Watergate scandal) tells of his personal journey from being a successful corporate lawyer to becoming someone who works on making leadership better for all of us. His story is both compelling and moving.

Johnson, Craig. *Meeting the Ethical Challenges of Leadership: Casting Light or Shadow.* Thousand Oaks, Calif.: Sage Publications, 2001. The author identifies the unique ethical demands of leadership and equips students to meet those challenges.

Jones, Laurie Beth. *The Path: Creating Your Mission Statement for Work and for Life.* New York: Hyperion, 1996. The author provides inspiring and practical advice to lead readers through every step of both defining and fulfilling a mission.

Kaye, Beverly, and Sharon Jordan-Evans. *Love 'Em or Lose 'Em: Getting Good People to Stay.* San Francisco: Berrett-Koehler, 2002. A thorough and well-written guidebook for managers who would like to keep good people in their employ.

Kotter, John P. *Leading Change.* Cambridge, Mass.: Harvard Business School Press, 1996. John Kotter's thesis is that strategies for change often fail in corporations because the changes do not alter behavior. He identifies the most common mistakes in effecting change, offering eight steps to overcoming obstacles.

Kouzes, James M., and Barry Z. Posner. *The Leadership Challenge.* San Francisco: Jossey-Bass, 1987. This is the flagship book for this talented team on what it really takes to be an effective serving leader.

Kretzmann, John P., and John L. McKnight. *Building Communities from the Inside Out: A Path Toward Finding and Mobilizing a Community's Assets.* Chicago: ACTA Publications, 1993. The authors guide readers to a new, asset-based approach to community building that proves everyone has a gift to share. The book offers practical advice, helpful tools, and powerful stories that help us see communities in new ways—as treasure troves of talent.

Letts, Christine W. *High Performance Nonprofit Organizations: Managing Upstream for Greater Impact.* New York: John Wiley and Sons, 1998. The author outlines approaches that nonprofits can use to build their capacity for learning, innovating, ensuring quality, and motivating staff.

Manz, Charles C. *The Leadership Wisdom of Jesus: Practical Lessons for Today.* San Francisco: Berrett-Koehler, 1999. The book focuses on practical, interpersonal management skills rather than visionary leadership. Charles Manz shows managers how to motivate and empower employees every day using the wisdom of Jesus.

Manz, Charles C., and Henry P. Sims Jr. *The New SuperLeadership: Leading Others to Lead Themselves.* San Francisco: Berrett-Koehler, 2001.

The book features numerous real-life stories of how leaders have achieved greater success by bringing out self-leadership in others.

Manz, Charles C., Karen P. Manz, Robert D. Marx, and Christopher P. Neck. *The Wisdom of Solomon at Work: Ancient Virtues for Living and Leading Today.* San Francisco: Berrett-Koehler, 2001. From biblical accounts of Job's faith, David's courage, Ruth's compassion, Moses' integrity, and Solomon's wisdom, readers learn how these personages faced obstacles similar to those today.

Nair, Keshavan. *A Higher Standard of Leadership: Lessons from the Life of Gandhi.* San Francisco: Berrett-Koehler, 1997. Dr. Keshavan Nair's genius is in illuminating the teachings of Gandhi, one of the greatest leaders of the twentieth century, and making them relevant to today's business world.

O'Neil, John R., and Jeremy Tarcher. *The Paradox of Success: When Winning at Work Means Losing at Life: A Book of Renewal for Leaders.* New York: G. P. Putnam's Sons, 1993. Inspires readers to look at failures, face the truth, and think of an action plan to make changes in life.

Paterson, Tom. *Living the Life You Were Meant to Live.* Nashville, Tenn.: Thomas Nelson, 1998. Inspirational step-by-step assessment process for life and vocation.

Perkins, John. *Restoring At-Risk Communities: Doing It Together and Doing It Right.* Grand Rapids, Mich.: Baker Book House, 1996. Perkins motivates people to become active members of their communities, providing a practical "how-to" guidebook for holistic community transformation.

Pollard, C. William. *Soul of the Firm.* Grand Rapids, Mich.: Zondervan, 2000. The author, chairman of the $3 billion ServiceMaster Company, believes that a commitment to people—employees as well as customers—is the reason for his corporation's continuous growth in revenue and profit during a quarter century.

Raelin, Joseph A. *Creating Leaderful Organizations: How to Bring Out Leadership in Everyone.* San Francisco: Berrett-Koehler, 2003. This book presents a new model of mutual leadership, which transforms leadership from one individual's responsibility into a new way of working for everyone.

Sashkin, Molly G., and Marshall Sashkin. *Leadership That Matters: The Critical Factors for Making a Difference in People's Lives and Organizations'*

Success. San Francisco: Berrett-Koehler, 2003. This book promotes leadership that improves productivity and performance and also makes a positive difference in the lives of organization members.

Senge, Peter. *The Fifth Discipline.* New York: Currency/Doubleday, 1994. The founder of the Center for Organizational Learning at MIT's Sloan School of Management coined the term "learning organization" in this seminal systems-thinking book.

Tichy, Noel M., and Eli B. Cohen. *The Leadership Engine.* San Francisco: HarperBusiness, 2002. *The Leadership Engine* is an outstanding, well-organized, and very readable book. Not just a book, it is a useful handbook as well. Noel Tichy includes a ninety-nine-page workbook with practical exercises designed both to help readers assess their own leadership and to help them develop a "Leadership Engine" in their own organization.

Tichy, Noel M., and Nancy Cardwell. *The Cycle of Leadership: How Great Leaders Teach Their Companies to Win.* San Francisco: HarperBusiness, 2002. The authors call on upper management to be more open, humble, and self-confident and to create an environment of teach and learn rather than the command-control approach of top-down management that has been prevalent since the machine age.

Wheatley, Margaret J. *Leadership and the New Science: Discovering Order in a Chaotic World.* Rev. San Francisco: Berrett-Koehler, 2001. This book explores the implications of quantum physics for organizational practice, then investigates ways that biology and chemistry affect living systems, and finally focuses on chaos theory, the creation of a new order, and the manner in which scientific principles affect leadership.

Wilkinson, Bruce. *The Prayer of Jabez: Breaking Through to the Blessed Life.* Sisters, Oreg.: Multnomah Publishers, 2000. Bruce Wilkinson challenges readers to recite the Jabez prayer every morning and keep a record of the changes that occur. The Greenwood prayer in our book is inspired by Wilkinson's story.

ABOUT THE AUTHORS

Ken Jennings, Ph.D.

Ken is the founder and managing partner of VentureWorks. He engages clients in the areas of leadership development, strategy, and the management of change. He is a senior advisor to Bethel University on Serving Leadership and executive development. Bethel is committed to creating a new and exciting approach to executive leadership development that combines the best of leadership coaching, strategy execution assistance, and servant leadership in action.

Ken has participated in multiple citywide initiatives aimed at accelerating the effective work of Serving Leaders in their communities. He has a passion for coaching executives to be more effective leaders while pursuing significance in their lives.

Ken was previously a senior partner at Accenture. He delivered client engagements in change management, strategy, postmerger integration, medical management, organizational transformation, team development, scenario planning, information systems implementation, and operations improvement. During those years, Ken worked with many of the leading companies in the country.

Prior to his work at Accenture, Ken served as a military officer around the world in various leadership roles. He is currently helping to build new technology companies in the homeland defense and biodefense fields.

He has taught at Wheaton College, the University of Michigan Business School, the Columbia University Business School, the University of Maryland (East Asian Division), the King's Fund College in London, and the Air Force Institute of Technology. His previous book, *Changing Health Care: Creating Tomorrow's Winning Health Enterprise*, focused on the key strategies used by leading health organizations to transform healthcare.

Ken holds a doctorate in organizational behavior from Purdue University, a master of science degree in management from the Air

Force Institute of Technology, and a bachelor of science degree in behavioral science from the United States Air Force Academy.

He most often resides at altitude on commercial jets or on-site with clients. Ken is happy to be contacted at (248) 761-0197 or at Ken.Jennings@ventureworks.org.

John Stahl-Wert, D.Min.

John is president and CEO of Pittsburgh Leadership Foundation (PLF), a twenty-five-year-old faith-based intermediary organization in Pittsburgh that specializes in bringing together leaders from the business, government, and social sectors to address human and social problems. John leads a staff of twenty-five diverse, multisector leaders who manage $12 million of annual work to improve the life conditions and self-sufficiency of the poor.

For nine years, John's work with Pittsburgh Leadership Foundation has involved creating new nonprofit organizations, establishing business-centric approaches to nagging social sector struggles, and training nonprofit executives in board management, partnership building, and social entrepreneurship.

John is also on the faculty of Geneva College's Masters of Science in Organizational Leadership, where he teaches in the area of ethics, decision making, and servant leadership. John's students are full-time working adults—leaders in many areas of business and human service—who bring to each class real-world leadership problems to solve.

Prior to becoming president of PLF, John founded and directed the national Council of Leadership Foundations Training Institute, working with leadership foundations in dozens of U.S. cities to strengthen their impact in their communities. John has taught widely in the area of social sector leadership and has given addresses at urban congresses in the United States as well as in Asia, Africa, and Latin America.

John is an ordained Mennonite pastor, currently assigned to provide oversight and support to other ministers. He holds a doctorate in transformational leadership from Eastern Baptist Theological Seminary, a master of arts degree in theological studies from Associated Mennonite Seminary, and a bachelor of science degree in sociology and social work from Eastern Mennonite University.

John has committed his lifetime to love and serve the city of Pittsburgh and its people. Most evenings, he can be found helping his wife cook dinner for his family or marveling at how quickly his children are growing.

WANT TO LEARN MORE?

Would you like to

- Connect to others who have read this book?
- Find a tool that will help you clarify your life purpose?
- Bring Serving Leadership into your business?
- Find a Serving Leader coach or a group you can join?
- Learn how to connect your business to your community?
- Hear more about Mike Wilson?
- Chat with the authors?

VISIT WWW.THESERVINGLEADER.COM

The authors' Web site will link you to the best practices in Serving Leadership and connect you to many other leaders who are practicing Serving Leadership in their teams and businesses, families, and communities.

Berrett-Koehler Publishers

B errett-Koehler is an independent publisher of books and other publications at the leading edge of new thinking and innovative practice on work, business, management, leadership, stewardship, career development, human resources, entrepreneurship, and global sustainability.

Since the company's founding in 1992, we have been committed to creating a world that works for all by publishing books that help us to integrate our values with our work and work lives, and to create more humane and effective organizations.

We have chosen to focus on the areas of work, business, and organizations, because these are central elements in many people's lives today. Furthermore, the work world is going through tumultuous changes, from the decline of job security to the rise of new structures for organizing people and work. We believe that change is needed at all levels—individual, organizational, community, and global—and our publications address each of these levels.

To find out about our new books,
special offers,
free excerpts,
and much more,
subscribe to our free monthly eNewsletter at

www.bkconnection.com

Please see next pages for other books
from Berrett-Koehler Publishers

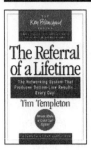

The Referral of a Lifetime
The Networking System That Produces Bottom-Line Results... Every Day!

Tim Templeton

Part of The Ken Blanchard Series, *The Referral of a Lifetime* teaches a step-by-step system that will allow anyone to generate a steady stream of new business through consistent referrals from existing customers and friends and, at the same time, maximize business with existing customers.

Hardcover • ISBN 1-57675-240-2 • Item #52402 $19.95

Your Leadership Legacy
The Difference You Make in People's Lives

Marta Brooks, Julie Stark, and Sarah Caverhill

Your leadership legacy is the sum total of the difference you make in people's lives, directly and indirectly, formally and informally. The challenge is how to live in a way that creates a legacy that will make a positive difference in the lives of those around you. *Your Leadership Legacy* shows you how to live a meaningful legacy.

Hardcover • ISBN 1-57675-287-9 • Item #52879 $19.95

Formula 2+2
The Simple Solution for Successful Coaching

Douglas Allen and Dwight Allen

Written in the accessible and compelling Blanchard storytelling style, *Formula 2+2* shows how to foster a culture of continuous feedback which increases the effectiveness of the manager, protects the spirit and dignity of employees, and provides a systematic approach to reinforcing and improving employee performance.

Hardcover, • ISBN 1-57675-310-7, Item #53107 $19.95

Berrett-Koehler Publishers
PO Box 565, Williston, VT 05495-9900
Call toll-free! **800-929-2929** 7 am-9 pm EST

Or fax your order to 1-802-864-7626
For fastest service order online: **www.bkconnection.com**

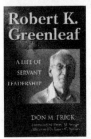

Robert K. Greenleaf
A Life of Servant Leadership

Don M. Frick

Formally authorized by Greenleaf's surviving children, this is the first biography of Robert K. Greenleaf, author of *Servant Leadership,* who first lived the servant-leader philosophy, created the term, and applied it to management and organizations.

Hardcover • ISBN 1-57675-276-3 • Item #52763 $29.95

The Power of Servant Leadership
Robert K. Greenleaf
Edited by Larry C. Spears

Based on the seminal work of Robert Greenleaf, *The Power of Servant Leadership* emphasizes an emerging approach to leadership that puts serving others first. This collection includes nine of Greenleaf's most compelling essays that contain many of his best insights.

Paperback • ISBN 1-57675-035-3 • Item #50353 $17.95

Leadership and Self-Deception
Getting Out of the Box

The Arbinger Institute

Leadership and Self-Deception reveals that there are only two ways for leaders to be: the source of leadership problems or the source of leadership success. The authors examine this surprising truth, identify self-deception as the underlying cause of leadership failure, and show how any leader can overcome self-deception to become a consistent catalyst of success.

Hardcover • 1-57675-094-9 • Item #50949 $22.00

Paperback • 1-57675-174-0 • Item #51740 $14.95

Berrett-Koehler Publishers
PO Box 565, Williston, VT 05495-9900
Call toll-free! **800-929-2929** 7 am-9 pm EST

Or fax your order to 1-802-864-7626
For fastest service order online: **www.bkconnection.com**

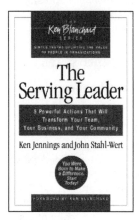